You've Been
Hoodwinked

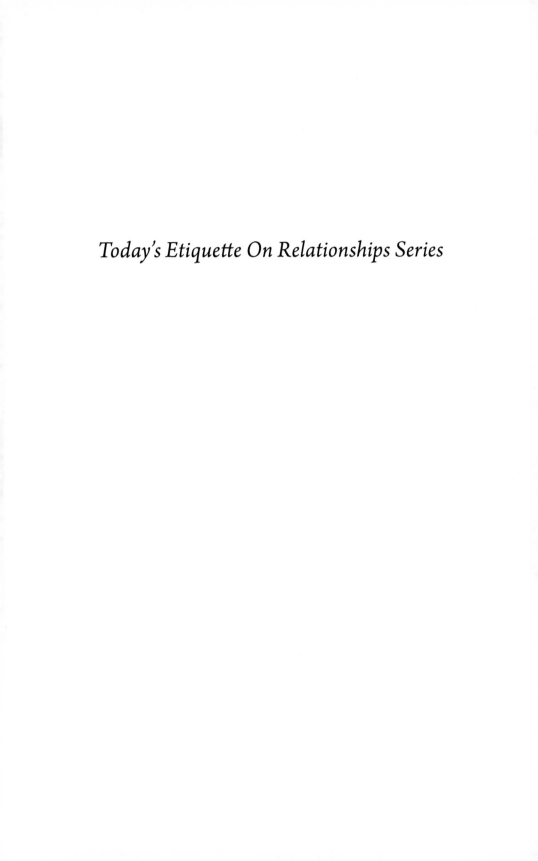

Today's Etiquette On Relationships Series

You've Been Hoodwinked Trial Part 1

Setting the record straight. Dispelling the myths about relationships which were created by the so-called expert. It's judgment day.

James B-More Wharton

You've Been Hoodwinked Trial Part 1

ISBN 978-0-9962989-0-2

Published by:
Wharton Enterprises, LLC
Ellenwood, Georgia 30294

DEDICATIONS

To: Edna Young, aka Granny

My loving mother and best friend. You've been with me through the good and bad times. You've been the only one I could rely on. Regardless of the circumstances, not once have you turned your back on me. You're the only one who has loved me regardless of my station in life. I will never put anything or anybody before you. You're the greatest gift this side of heaven.

I cherish you not only because of your commitment to me, but also because I must follow the command Jesus uttered on the cross as one of his last seven words: *"Woman, behold thy son . . . And son, behold thy* mother . . ." (John 19:26–27). I will behold you even unto the end of the earth.

—Baby Boy

CONTENTS

FOREWORD

THE 21ST CENTURY'S solution for meeting someone to date is, not surprisingly enough, electronic courting. Dating websites are a popular but expensive means for initiating a possible relationship. Most of these websites mislead individuals with a "free" profile. Some allow free searches and smiles or winks, but if the person wishes to send an email or a message, they have to purchase a membership. There are some free websites, but from personal experience, the only contact I've received is from spammers or guys who live in another state.

In his book, *You've Been Hoodwinked,* James Wharton gives a detailed look at how problems with dating have emerged in our society over the decades. He explains the historical customs of a boy's transition into manhood and how the influence of the media, technology, and those who want to benefit financially from the innocent use seemingly unblemished ways to pollute the minds and emotions of others.

The author uses biblical scripture to authenticate the truth in building positive relationships. He includes information on the emotional, intellectual, and spiritual differences between a boy and a man. Anyone who is single, divorced, or widowed would benefit from reading this book. It will enlighten you on the basics of a healthy relationship and the caution signs along the way.

~ Melody Ravert
Author of *Heaven or Hell: The Choice is Yours* and *My Special Angel: Raising a Child with Autism as a Single Parent*
www.melodyravert.com

PREFACE

But they that wait upon the Lord shall renew their strength;
they shall mount with wings as eagles; they shall run, and
not be weary; and they shall walk, and not faint.

(ISAIAH 40:31)

THE TOPIC OF relationships are permeating our society in a pandemic way. Everyone seems to be an expert on the topic. From the water-cooler expert counselor to the celebrity comedian, radio talk show host, and television personality, you can find some of the most ridiculous theories on relationships ever concocted. Some of these theories are so preposterous, it makes one wonder, if those who are wafting them out of their mouths believe in these theories themselves—it sounds like they're talking out of the side of their necks.

Some even think they're an expert on relationships because of the letters behind their names (e.g., PhD). On the contrary, I believe there's only one relationship expert in the history of mankind—he can solve every issue we face in our relationships. He has written a God–Help Book that is guaranteed to work if its principles are applied properly. Any other book penned that doesn't coincide with His book is a no-help book.

I am not a relationship expert. Thus, as a result of my lack of carnal educational expertise with relationships, many will question my authority to speak on relationships. In other words, who gives me the right to speak on such a complex topic?

Although I am not a relationship expert, I am employed by the one and only relationship expert known to man: God. I am His ambassador. I graduated from the University of Hard Knocks with a GED (God Educational Doctorate) in the Father, Son, and Holy Spirit. I have been licensed to proclaim His doctrines on relationships since the year 2000, and I have done my due diligence in the studying of his relationship-help manuscript. Further, I have proven to have the intellectual, experiential, and practical knowledge to dialogue on the unquestionable spiritual principles He has prescribed for relationships. I will only speak on those things I have first-hand knowledge to and believe with all my heart, mind, body, and soul. And trust me, it's not my business to give heretical testimony. I have a first-hand account of the events in question.

> *As God's agent, He has given me the authority, power, and ability to speak on the oracles of His word: And Jesus came and spake unto them, saying, All Power is given unto me in heaven and in earth. Go ye therefore, and teach all nations, baptizing them in the name of the Father, and of the Son, and of the Holy Ghost: Teaching them to observe all things whatsoever I have commanded you: and, lo, I am with you always, even unto the end of the world. Amen.*
> (MATTHEW 28:19–20)

As one can see, I have some serious backup. They're at the top of their field of study, and their sources are infallible. I come highly recommended and equipped for the task at hand.

Further, as an ambassador for the relationship expert, I am obligated to speak on the things He tells me to speak on—even if it means pulling the covers off my own character flaws and defects (Corinthians 5:20). No sugar will be added to this Kool-Aid.

The Bible will be my go-to source for refuting the erroneous statements of the unlearned. The Bible is a collection of works that cover every field of study: relationships, science, engineering, and, yes, homosexuality and masturbation is covered as well. You name it, it's in the Good Book.

At present, I have in my possession a copy of those documents. This compilation of books has been the number-one bestseller since its inception. It is sold both nationally and globally. Its translations are vast—and its wisdom is unmatched. No other book in the history of mankind can make such a claim. None!

God has summoned me to annihilate the fallacies committed by those who give hearsay testimony and practice false divination. Arrest them, prosecute them, convict them, and sentence them for the heinous crimes committed against His word.

During the course of this trial, God has provided me with expert witnesses who will testify on His behalf. These witnesses will be revealed in the case briefing in a soon-to-come section of this indictment.

I do understand studying the Bible can be time consuming and difficult. It takes great patience, training, discipline, and passion to understand the precepts of scholastic writings. Peter, in his second epistle, expressed his difficulty in understanding the lofty writings of Paul, the great apostle—one of the greatest philosophical minds of all times (2 Peter 3:16).

Much like Paul's writings, the Bible is written in a language and fashion that can be difficult and frustrating to the reader. This is why God has chosen a select few who have the discipline, training, patience, passion, and ability to rightfully divide His word (God's Special Forces). One must have more than a basic understanding of the precepts of God to effectively contemporize his message. God is a complicated man, and no one understands him but his children—The Bloods of Christ.

So no one will be mistaken about my intent, let me be perfectly clear. I have been set for the defense of the Gospel of Jesus Christ: *"The one preach Christ of contention, not sincerely, supposing to add affliction to my bonds: But the other of love, knowing that I am set for the defense of the Gospel"* (Philippians 1:16–17).

I intend to destroy the book the so-called expert has written and the false principles on which it stands. The bar will be set so high every so-called relationship counselor will have no choice but to seek the Bible for guidance. These books will be taken off of bookshelves, left to collect dust, trashed, or thrown in the back window of the readers' cars with their Bibles. Better yet, just burn them.

As a Christian and a defender of God's Word, when the so-called relationship experts spew things that are lethal and contradictory to God's Word, I must take quick and decisive action to repudiate the atrocities committed by such individuals. I cannot just sit by idly and let things just be. Why? The Bible says, *"Death and Life are in the tongue . . ."* (Proverbs 18:21). Therefore, if I just sit on the seat of do nothing, I am just as guilty as those who are pulling the trigger. I am guilty through the whole process of the crime: during the commission of the crime, and after the crime— guilty. There is no two ways about it.

The aforementioned charges carry very stiff penalties. I can be sentenced to death or life in prison without the possibility of parole. I'm not about to let that happen just to spare the egos and feelings of a few who think they're privileged. It is from this angle that I am writing this book.

I am fully aware there will be those who will disagree with some of the contents of this book—some will even argue with the Bible—and that's okay. It is their God-given and constitutional right to do so. However, I intend to back up everything I state in this book by the canonical scriptures. This book's angle will be validated with ease and by using only a fraction of biblical text.

On the one hand, I am not concerned about grown folk. You make your bed hard, you lie in it. Experience is the best teacher. On the other hand, I am concerned. I understand we are all on different levels of thinking. This is not to say I am intellectually superior to anyone. I just know some of us don't like to study, and that's not okay.

We must always keep in mind the importance of becoming familiar with the instructions of the Bible. If not, we will never be able to lead our children in the way they should go. Our children will continue on a path of destruction that may be insurmountable. If blind leaders are permitted to lead our children, we will find ourselves in a situation where the spiritually blind will be leading the spiritually blind, and we all know where that will lead us. Just look around and see for yourself.

Note: If one has not been shown or taught the way to go—or, if one has been taught but forgotten the way to go—how can they give directions to someone else?

Think on this for a second: Our forefathers and foremothers may not have had the education we have, but you must agree, what little they did have, they used it well and it brought us a mighty long way. As a result, we can never underestimate the value of being in tune with our surroundings. Our foremothers demonstrated this fact in their ability to determine if a man was good for them or not. Just check out the illustration of a Lady verses a Girl that will be presented in a later count of this case.

Conversely, I am extremely concerned about our future generations of young men and women. We cannot continue to perpetuate the same behaviors and expect to achieve different results—that's what they call insanity. Children must be taught the way they should go. And the lack of judgment exercised by those whom I oppose is clear evidence something must be done.

Here is some food for thought: *"The fear of the Lord is the beginning of knowledge: but fools despise wisdom and instruction. . . ."* (Proverbs 1:7). In the words of some of the most famous negro philosophers, who go by the names RUN, DMC, and JAM MASTER JAY—so-called expert, "you talk too much, and then you never shut up: Shut up!"

Remember, the greatest asset God has given us is our ability to *think*. So *think!* Don't take anything for *face value*. Don't believe what people say just because they sound good and think they know it all. Do your own research and find out for yourself. Don't be duped by the cloak of intelligence—not even for your beloved pastor. History tells us that even Jesus had to prove His deity to the people. So why not test the validity of the flamboyant rhetoric of an impostor.

It's my prayer that everyone who reads this book will find something between these pages they can use—even those whom I am disputing. If not, at least open the Bible more than on Sunday and see for yourself. That's the least one can do in order to stay in the right lane.

I promise, as sure as God lives, I will tell the truth, the whole truth, and nothing but the truth, so help me . . . while at the same time trying to perhaps put a smile on someone's face in hopes of changing their life. May God continue to bless you, and may heaven always shine its face upon you. Read well.

Don't worry. Be happy. Help is on the way.

THE SUPREME COURT
OF THE MOST HIGH

THE HOST OF HEAVEN

V.

THE SO-CALLED RELATIONSHIP EXPERTS

LITIGANTS

The People of God, Plaintiffs

The So-Called Relationship Expert, Defendant

SYNOPSIS: The Host of Heaven has accused the defendant of spiritual murder, attempted spiritual murder, providing hearsay testimony, practicing false divination, reckless endangerment, witchcraft, theft by deception, impersonating an expert relationship counselor, malicious destruction, armed robbery, misleading vulnerable women, using God's name in vain, misappropriating God's word, practicing without a license, promoting adultery and fornication, discounting the many years of experiential insight a mother has regarding a man's mind, and not practicing what they preach.

FACTS: Plaintiffs – The defendant has written a book that's been distributed nationwide. Many women have used the defendant's methods and have found them to be a complete failure. Scholars, theologians, and clergy have read the defendant's book and have found it to be only useful in starting their fireplaces. The accused doctrines are based on heathenish beliefs and practices. The doctrines of the defendant's book undermine God's authority, wisdom, and His supreme deity. Because of a lack of prudence, this book has caused a great deal of unnecessary heartache, confusion, and disappointment when the doctrines of this book were tried at home by women.

FACTS: Defendant – This book has been written by some of the foremost leaders in the field of relationship counseling. Satan, the Father of lies, Beelzebub; athletes; ex-cons and hustlers; movie and television stars; ministers and deacons are all contributors this magnificent piece of work. These writers are some of the most upstanding citizens this side of heaven. Their information is ironclad and can be applied to anyone's lifestyle. We believe only a quarter of a brain is needed for someone to apply our principles. Therefore, if someone gets it wrong, it's not our problem. Besides, they were warned by God of such books and didn't read the fine print or handwriting on the wall before purchasing our books. We are absolutely free of any liability, because we were only doing what we do—lie.

LEGAL ISSUE: Plaintiffs – We know that the writing of these books is a direct contradiction of God's laws. They promote a licentious lifestyle and deny the precedence God has established even before the foundation of the earth. Furthermore, these books make a mockery of the institutions God holds dear to His heart. They mutilate God's character and smear His Holy name. They create confusion for babes in Christ and cause them undue heartache and pain.

LEGAL ISSUE: Defendant – We feel the plaintiffs' case bares no merit since we follow heathenish practices. Heathenish practices are the standards by which all men should live. They provide us with all the essential elements needed for a happy life. All the women we want, money, nice cars and houses, and all the fame a man could ever want. God's laws only apply to people of Old Time and those who want to follow them if they feel like it. Even though we claim God occasionally, we're not obligated to waste our time with them age-old traditions. Those traditions are for the birds. You can hardly understand them anyway. Our time is better spent chasing the almighty dollar—what has Jesus done for us lately? He is never on time and comes when he feels like it. The story about Jesus getting up from the grave is false, and, therefore, his contract is null and void.

REMEDY SOUGHT: Plaintiffs – We are asking the court that the defendants be prevented from ever speaking on the topic of relationships—pay restitutions to each individual they stole money from—be given a life sentence to cultivating their own back yards— stop practicing adultery and honor the wives they have—they take off the cloak of sin—they issue a public apology to the people they deceived—they take all their books and put them in a pile and burn them—and they be sentence to a lifetime of community service for the betterment of women.

REMEDY SOUGHT: Defendant – We are asking the court to instruct the plaintiffs to mind their own business and get up off our back so we can make all the money we can; it's none of their business. Allow us to do whatever we want, whenever we want, and however we want, regardless of the harm it may bring to God's people. We can do damned well as we please, and if people don't like it, to hell with them. If someone is foolish enough to believe in our false doctrines, that's on them. We are not anybody's role model. That's Mama's and Daddy's responsibility. As the defendants, our responsibility is to no one but ourselves. We've never read in the Bible that we are accountable to anyone.

CASE PROFILE

PRESIDING JUDGES: The Father, Son, and the Holy Spirit

PROSECUTING ATTORNEY: James B-More Wharton

DEFENSE ATTORNEY: Satan

JURY: The Apostles of Jesus

PLANTIFFS' EXPERT WITNESSES: Adam and Eve; Moses; Shade Rack, Meshach, and Abednego; Daniel in the lion's den; Job; the Twelve Tribes of Judah; Paul; and John the Baptist.

DEFENDANT'S EXPERT WITNESSES: Judas; Lucifer; Jezebel; Delilah; Baal; pimps, hustlers, and ex-cons; mortgage and insurance brokers; professional athletes, movie and television stars; the very men women are complaining about.

BAILIFFS: The Angels of God with flaming swords

Note: Due to the need to preserve space, I cannot give a complete exposition on every character mentioned in this case profile. To see the importance of each character, some understanding of biblical history will be needed. If one doesn't know already, here's a list of some aids that may help: Bible, Concordance of the Bible, Commentary of the Bible, Bible Dictionary, etc.

We will need some understanding of God's laws to be able to follow the evidence that will be presented in this monumental case. This case is a matter of life and death. And the life you might save may be yours.

> *Study to show thyself approved unto God, a workman that needeth not to be ashamed, rightly dividing the word of truth. But shun profane and vain babblings: for they will increase unto more ungodliness. . . .*
>
> (2 TIMOTHY 2:15–16)

So let's study.

QUIET PLEASE
COURT IS NOW IN SESSION

OPENING ARGUMENTS

DEFENSE ATTORNEY: Satan

INTEND TO PROVE that the charges against my clients are unfounded, trumped-up, bare no merit, and only serve to do harm to my client's stellar reputation. The stories against me and the clients I represent are frivolous. I wasn't kicked out of heaven—I was God's beloved angel. Judas didn't betray Jesus—everybody lied on him because they were jealous of him. Delilah and Jezebel were two of the finest women you ever want to meet. My clients who wrote on relationships were following God's Law with the strictest adherence—they helped many people live a prosperous life here on earth even though their marriages ended in divorce. My clients only had their best interest at heart. They have a heart for God—and God only told them half the story.

PROSECUTING ATTORNEY: James B-More Wharton

WILL PROVE BEYOND a shadow of doubt that what you just heard is a bunch of bull crap. The defense attorney is a liar and the father of lies. Those whom he represents are his children. They're his cohorts and intend to make a mockery of God's Holy ordinances. They will do anything for money—their love for money is so great, they will risk the lives of their own children. They're perpetrating a fraud and won't even practice what they preach—and they deserve to receive the maximum punishment allowed by law.

Note: Some of the defense's witnesses couldn't appear in court today because they're probably lying up with someone's wife just as I am speaking.

Others may be out robbing stores on their way back from work release. And some may be in church laying hands on women in all the wrong places. At this time, Most Holy, I would like to submit into evidence a copy of the manuscript you left behind for all to see. It will be labeled as prosecution exhibit, the one and only: THE BIBLE.

COUNT 1

LADYMAN

And Adam said, This is now bone of my bone, and flesh of my flesh:
she shall be called Woman, because she was taken out of Man.
—GENESIS 2:23

FROM THE OUTSET, even the title of this book is flawed. In his opening statement to this count, the defendant consistently uses the word *woman* to describe the female. However, throughout the defendant's entire book, the reference to a lady is used with great infrequency. One must use a fine toothed comb to locate the word *lady*. The most high-powered microscope would have difficulty identifying the word *lady* in the defendant's book.

Only to some surprise, most of us know there is an enormous difference between a woman and a lady; further, being a lady is not an act by any stretch of the imagination. Actors and actresses act. They go into character and become the personalities of the characters they're portraying. Being a lady does not work like that in real life. A woman is either a lady or not.

A woman who is not a true lady will never be able to pull off a performance to completely convince her audience she is a lady. At some point, the performance will come apart at the seams, and she will do something that will reveal her true identity by overwhelming evidence. Her legs will pop open in front of a group of strange men, she will bend over in public with her tail to the sky for all to see, she will reach down into her bosom to retrieve something—the costume of a lady will become irritating and she will disrobe piece by piece pulling the covers off herself. Thereby, revealing her true identity.

Now that the lady perpetrator has achieved the level of physical and psychological comfort she is accustomed to, her mouth will began to take over and put the nail in the coffin. Her speech will turn unbecoming of a lady, and she will engage in conversations with her male counterparts that a real lady would never even fathom. Further, after revealing her true nature to those around her, when approached like anything but a lady, she will react with great dismay and utter surprise—not accepting the fact that she let the cat out of the bag.

On the contrary, and in a galaxy far away, it is not necessary for a true lady to perform an act. Being a lady is so ingrained in her it comes natural. It is who she is, and it stands out like a sore thumb. Moreover, with little observation a true man will recognize a true lady after being in her presence for a short time—she will have "true lady" written all over her face. No one in her presence will be mistaken by what she stands for. Her uniform will be stellar from head to toe, and even the other women in her presence will have to take notice: *Girl, where did you get that outfit from; I ain't never seen no hook-up like that; I wish I could dress like that; shoot, all the fine men were looking at you.*

The 4-1-1: A true lady is defined by her character. And yes, her appearance is a part of her character. She doesn't have to put on an act for anyone. She's comfortable in her own skin, and she doesn't have to validate her lady-hood to anyone, especially not to the defendant in this case. A true lady's character is habitual, and she needs no script to follow. Her lady-hood will shine as bright as the stars illuminating the sky. She has received extensive training from her mother at the Mothers School for Training a Girl into Lady-Hood, where their motto is "Be a lady at all times."

My sisters, once again, you're either a lady or not. It is what it is. If you have failed to meet the required standards for graduating from the

University of Lady-Hood, you can take some summer classes at your community college to bring you up to standards. If you are willing to put in the extra work required to smooth out your rough edges, I am one hundred percent confident that you and every other woman can graduate from the University of Lady-Hood.

Note: What constitutes a lady verses a woman is on two different ends of the spectrum. It's like a fish out of water, a peanut-butter-and-jelly sandwich without the jelly, Curley without Larry and Moe. Therefore, some examples of the differences between a lady and a girl stuck in a woman's body will be further exemplified in a later section. Take careful note of these examples if you flunked out of the University of Lady-Hood.

A WOMAN'S NATURE

FIRST, AND OF foremost importance, women are women because of their relationship to man—hence, womb-man. This noted fact by nature makes her a man with minimum differences. She is called such because she was taken out of man; we all know the story. God caused a deep sleep to fall upon Adam . . . and He took a rib. . . . The end.

On the other hand, according to our legal system, a girl becomes a woman when she reaches a certain age. By this standard, and in most states, the only thing required for a girl to become a woman is to live until she reaches the age of eighteen. After that, she is entitled to do whatever she wants, whenever she wants, and however she wants—she's a woman.

Secondly, thinking like a man on the outside sounds profound, but when searched out, it's nothing but tinkling brass. Furthermore, since a woman is considered a man with a womb, why would it be necessary for her to try to think like a man-woman? She is Man-kind. She possesses all the faculties a man possesses. And yes, that includes thinking.

When God created Eve she came with all the essential characteristics of her male counterpart and nothing was left out. In other words, God made her compatible to man, just like him. She can think, lead, manage, make decisions. And this might surprise some, but she can walk and chew bubble gum at the same time. Can I get a witness?

The differences between a man and a woman are so minute only a fool couldn't see them. By the way, I hope I'm not the only man who notices we have a lot of women in high places. Some are in Congress, some are CEO's of major corporations, and many are the heads of their households. And I don't have a problem being a stay-home dad. My manhood won't be hurt at all. Are there any ladies out there looking for a husband to stay home and take care of the kids—I'm here for you.

My Skills: I change pampers; wash clothes; do dishes; run bath water; iron the children's clothes; get the kids dressed; take them to school; cook; rub feet, backs, and toes—you name it and I can do it.

God's creation, please don't be amazed by those who speak profane and babbling words. Take the advice Paul gave to Timothy and turn away from words that are meaningless and devoid of truth—a bunch of hot air.

In closing to this count, even if a woman's thinking is different than that of a man, she possesses enough empirical and intellectual knowledge of a man's mind to effectively cohabitate with her man to the end of a successful relationship. After all, she got her mind from a man. Now don't forget the adage, my sisters, "Mama always knows best." She is your best ally when trying to understand a man's mind. She will never steer you wrong.

Word to the wise: Learn to examine your food before you eat it. And please always take into consideration the reputation of the cook who's preparing your food. You don't want a short-order cook attempting to prepare a gourmet meal for you. Your order will turn out to be a disaster you will never forget. *WOMB-MAN POWER.* Think like a man, sisters . . . because you are a man.

Everything You Need to Know About Boys and Relationships is in Steve's Book

THE FIRST THING that stands out to me in the count of this book's hypocrisy is the author's boasting of his wisdom, knowledge, and the value of his self-proclaimed ability to instruct women on the proper etiquette for getting the man of their dreams. We all know that man's wisdom and intellect is but a dot on the wall compared to God's wisdom. There's no comparing the two.

> *And my speech and preaching was not with enticing words of man's wisdom, but in demonstration of the Spirit and of power. That your faith should not stand in the wisdom of men, but in the power of God.*
>
> (1 CORINTHIANS 2:4–5)

Personally, I find man's claim to wisdom above God's wisdom to be satanic. Only Satan and his demons believe their wisdom is above God's. That's the exact thing that caused Satan to be expelled from heaven: his wisdom. I think I'm going to take my chances on the wisdom of the One who created me. It seems to me if He made me, then He should know how to fix me. So why take a chance with someone who wouldn't know truth if the truth sat down on a bus next to him and said, "Hi, I'm the truth; it's nice to meet you."

Just as insulting, the defendant boldly and emphatically demeans some women's ability to think. "Too many women are clueless," he says. It shouldn't take a rocket scientist to see his use and tone of the word *clueless* is basically calling some women stupid.

To give you the 4-1-1, not knowing something doesn't equate to being stupid. Being stupid is when a woman knows a man is a dog and still hooks up with him. On the contrary, some men have practiced doggish ways so much they have it down to a science. It is usually only after a woman has been with a man for a certain length of time that she discovers he's a dog. That's not stupid. By the way, I wonder what type of women the defendant has been dealing with—stupid or not?

In my lifetime, I have met some very intelligent women. Not only are they intellectually astute, but they are very adept at identifying a man from a boy. Only women who haven't been schooled by their mothers at the art of boy identification would have difficulty distinguishing a man from a boy. The clueless ladies I have spoken with have identified the defendant I am prosecuting as having all the trimmings of a boy. I concur with their assessment.

Even more insulting, he discounts a mother's ability to teach her daughter how to distinguish a man from a boy. He wants women to forget everything their mothers ever taught them about men and listen to him— to stop listening to the ancient methods employed by mothers centuries ago, because they don't work. That's pretty bold.

Only someone who is suffering from an idiopathic condition would challenge the intellectual and experiential knowledge a mother has regarding a man's mind. You know if you let the cat out in the yard with a dog, the dog will devour the cat. I'm just saying.

I think mothers are the best resource a woman can find to get into the mind of a man. Experience is the best teacher. We cannot replace the knowledge our mothers have gained about the mind of a man and replace it with the fatuous statements that recklessly spew out of the mouth of one who is completely illiterate to God's word.

In times past, some of our mothers may not have had the book knowledge we have, but they had the wherewithal to distinguish a man from a boy. As my grandmother would say, "He's nothing but a good-for-nothing heathen." And she was right on the money with her fifth grade education.

Our foremothers had such a keen sense of awareness when it came to observing a man's behavior to determine his true identity, one can only shake their head in amazement. They looked for signs such as the following to determine if a man of interest were a man or boy-man:

BOY INDENTIFIERS

▸ Does he flaunt his stuff when he is around other women?

▸ Is the topic of the conversation about him?

▸ Does he look at every woman that passes him like they're a piece of meat?

▸ Is he a rolling stone? You all know the song.

▸ Does he have children all over the place by different women?

▸ Does he talk like every woman wants him—like he's God's gift?

▸ Does he brag about his things? House, money, clothing, and cars?

▸ Does he try to impress by attempting to use fancy words? Words he can't spell or define.

▸ Does he boast about who he knows? Athletes, doctors, movie stars, etc.?

▸ Does he dress like a pimp in loud, colorful suits and want to be seen by everybody?

▸ Does he brag about how good he is in the bed? (For three minutes ...)

▸ Does his conversation carry a sexual overtone?

▸ Does he know the difference between having sex and making love?

S o, a s y o u can see, our foremothers weren't stupid at all. They had more wisdom packed in one finger than the accused could begin to fathom in his pea-brain of a mind.

Women, if you don't have a relationship with your mother, if possible, develop one. She will take you on a journey through a man's mind you will never believe. And trust me, she will never steer you wrong. You can take that to the bank of wisdom and cash it; the check won't bounce.

Note: If it ain't broke, ladies, don't fix it. Let well enough alone.

Next, everything the indicted identified as being the desires of women are not exclusive to women, nor are women foolish to expect an equal effort from men. Many men seek most if not all of the same things women seek. Unfortunately, society has told men that if they reveal a compassionate side, they will be deemed less than a man.

As I stated earlier, a woman is cut from the cloth of a man. Therefore, she is only asking a man to give her what he gave her.

As such, she is perfectly within her right to expect a man to reciprocate her love.

So, if a woman is crazy to expect a man to reciprocate her love, men need to call God and tell Him He made a mistake in His design. Is there anyone out there who is big and bad enough to take on that challenge? It sure isn't going to be me.

The sentiments of equal output are painted on several pages of the Bible. And I know this may be surprising to some, especially the accused: The law of equal treatment is a command and not an option. This means a man is supposed to give to a woman exactly what she gives to him. Same love, same attention, same affection—same everything. Moreover, I don't profess to know everything there is to know about men, but as much as most men want to deny it, I believe most men deny their likeness to women out of pride and some age-old tradition that states: If a man admits to liking anything that is supposed to be exclusive to a woman, he will be viewed as being "Soft as Butter," and his manhood will be challenged by society.

Putting all false pretenses aside, I believe most sensible men want from women some, if not all, of the same things women openly express they want from men: Men want commitment; men want romance; men want to cuddle; men have hopes for a family; and men present the same complexity in their personality as their female counterparts. Going a little further, some men have more drama issues than women and present some of the very same challenges. Have you ever heard a woman tell a man to stop acting like a woman? I have. And as much as men would like to cover it up, I know from experience that a lot of men gossip just as much as women do, if not more. Now, isn't gossip something that is supposed to be exclusive to women? Hmmm, makes you wonder!

So, to even suggest certain things are exclusively pertaining to women is not worth the ink and pen used to write this phallic claim. When I discuss the reasons God created Adam for Eve, you will clearly see how impossible it is for a man to be absent of the same wishes and feelings of a woman.

In addition, according to the accused's idea of the journey to manhood, the search for manhood will never change nor end. Men will always seek a prey to devour. This concept is illustrated in his hole-ridden piece on "Men Like to Hunt"—a topic coming up soon.

Note: Finding manhood isn't a lifetime adventure. God built the world in seven days. If a man is of a certain age and he hasn't transitioned into manhood, it's more likely than not that the change will never take place.

My Transition to Manhood: I can testify to the blessing of allowing change to be a part of one's life. For instance, I'm not the same person I was when I moved to Georgia seventeen years ago. What a blessing that is! Many of my friends ask me why I don't get back with my ex-wife. It's simple. I'm not the same person I was seventeen years ago; I've changed. I'm a different man now. I think as a man is supposed to think—and I have a new thinking cap on.

Therefore, the type of woman I'm attracted to is much different than yesterday. What I want out of a relationship is different; the things I look for in a woman are different; what pleased me yesterday doesn't please me today; and it goes without saying, every woman doesn't meet my standards or God's standards for being my woman. No change. No progress.

Let's make something clear here. That last statement is not to say anything negative about my ex-wife. She is a great woman. If I had to do it all over again, I would still pick her as the mother of my child. She did a great job at raising my daughter. I'm just different now.

The defendant goes on to further state, "Women only fit into the cracks of his life"—*Fit into the cracks.* A woman doesn't fit into the cracks of a man's life; she's one flesh with him. She shares equal headship with her husband. I know that last statement is contrary to some people's church doctrine, but I'm going to leave that for another class.

Note: If the ideology of fitting into the cracks of a man's life isn't the way a boy thinks, I don't know what is. Remember, the Great Apostle Paul said: *"when I was a child ... but when I became a man ..."* You decide—child or man? Let the church say amen.

Listen to this and see if you get what I get: "Women must deal with men on their terms and they can take it or leave it. And if they don't like the crack their fitting into, they can hit the road Jill and don't you come back no more. I'm doing you a favor by allowing you to be with me—I'm the man."

This is all news to me. I thought a relationship operated on equal ground. My bad. I didn't know everything went my way, when I say it, and how I say it. I've been missing out on something. You ladies have been cheating me. Get over here and fix my dinner, woman. That's what it sounds like to me. I've been sleeping on my manly duties.

This statement puts women in a subservient role to men. She is beneath him and must obey his every command. It's sad to see the defendant use some of the same tactics many biblical scholars have used for centuries to oppress women. Fortunately, a lot of women have risen above this misappropriated biblical practice and are reaching for heights anyone in their right frame of mind could applaud with great joy.

I believe both the man and the woman should come to the middle of the road with their standards and see if they can be woven together.

If not, no hard feelings. Just keep it moving and hope to have better luck the next time.

This chauvinistic male mentality only works on woman who have a low self-esteem and are gullible enough to enter into such a demeaning situation. No woman with the least bit of integrity would subject themselves to being used as a doormat.

Fitting into the cracks of someone's life is like smearing joint compound into the cracks of a wall. After you get the joint compound into the wall, it is hidden. Moreover, joint compound is one of the cheapest products of the house. It has no voice, has no flexibility, can easily be replaced, cannot be seen or heard—and the position remains the same for the life of the house. That's got to be attractive to women. What do you say?

Heck, if fitting into the cracks of someone's life is a good thing, I know a few women whom I would like to be their joint compound. They can smear me all over them, hide me in the closet until they come home, fix me a cheap peanut butter and jelly sandwich for dinner, be my voice when we're making love, replace me by calling me a different name, and my position don't ever have to change. Yes. That's right! Call me Daddy Joint Compound. Can I get an amen?

Only to some dismay, I have met some ladies who were pretty affluent at expressing their thoughts—and they did not have a problem with letting a man know what standards they live by. In fact, I dated a woman who was cloaked with intelligence. She could talk for me anytime. I used to just sit there and enjoy seeing her operate, not saying a mumbling word. And guess what, I didn't feel less than a man. Why? Because that was my baby and seeing her operate turned me on, made me proud, and gave me the assurance that, outside of my presence, she wasn't about to let anyone push her over. Also, it told me if I was on my sick bed and couldn't make a decision for myself, I knew I had a woman by me who had the ability to decide for me. She wouldn't sit there like a chicken with its head chopped off and let the doctors tell her any old thing. Does that sound like *fitting in the cracks* to you?

Attention Ladies: Let that last fact sink in deep. This is a trait real men look for in a woman: the ability to decide. Breast and booty may attract a real man to you, but it's not going to be the deciding factor. You must come to the table with more than your body.

Furthermore, in my entire life, I have never been a soft man. I know when a man is supposed to step in and take over for his woman. And trust me, when I step, I step.

A Woman Fits into the Womb of a Man's Heart

T HE HEART IS a very small organ in the body. However, the power the heart possesses is unmatchable. It is the engine that makes sure everything works properly. It lubricates, replenishes, protects, defends, and supplies every other organ in the body with the needed oxygen. Without the heart, all will cease to exist.

To a man, a woman functions very much the same way a heart functions to the body. She pumps lifeblood into the man. She supplies oxygen to the many cells contained within a man to assist him with sustaining life—and she supplies confidence, companionship, a listening ear, troubleshooting, and, yes, Mrs. fix-it skills. A woman listens to the details of a man's trivial problems, and through her love, she leaps into action with her Wonder Woman cape on to save her man from whatever is endangering him. Sadly, she is rejected by the pride of an ancient historical practice which says a man is the only one who can fix it.

My sisters, don't be duped, men need everything you need—including help fixing things. Unfortunately for some men, they're just too proud to admit it. Consequently, some relationships suffer undue hardship because of a man undermining a woman's ability to do something that we think is reserved for a man.

Even more disturbing in this case is how the defendant compares a relationship to a game—a playbook. Boys consider a relationship a game, but not men. If you ask me, this is the leading cause of confusion in relationships—games. A relationship is not a game. It is extremely serious business. It shouldn't be taken lightly and must be done with some idea of what a relationship really entails. So, let me help all the boys out there understand the dynamics of a relationship.

A relationship is a partnership. As such, each partner has equal authority in the decision-making process of the partnership. No one party is the ruling authority. Each member must be included in the affairs of the partnership to maintain cohesiveness. No one member should make decisions without first consulting the other partner. If one party makes a decision without the other, this violates the trust clause in the relationship contract and creates discord within the relationship. And we all know discord within a relationship causes grave concern to the non-violating partner, and in some cases, they would be rightfully justified in dissolving the relationship. For example, cheating, stealing, and lying are acts that can cause the dissolution of a relationship. However, these traits are blatantly promoted and are the tenants by which the defendant's ideology of a man stands.

When the trust clause is violated in a relationship (whatever type of relationship it may be), most relationships never recover. Why? Trust is the most important product of a relationship. When violated, the non-violating party is devastated, and the act that caused the distrust is etched in their mind forever. They can never get rid of it, no matter what they do. As a result, the non-violating party would be under no obligation to perform the remainder of the contract: contract null and void. Now that's a crack the ladies I know would never try to fit into.

If done in the way God intended for it to be done, a relationship can be a beautiful experience for both parties involved. However, too many people take relationships for granted, like it's a joke or a challenge to play with someone's mind.

For instance, while talking on the phone to a woman I was considering dating, I remember her telling me to bring my A-game when I met her for dinner. After that statement, I really didn't want to go. Why? I don't have a game. I refuse to play with a woman's feelings. It is my custom to lay my intentions on the line from the very beginning. If I'm not looking for a relationship, I will let the woman know up front so she can choose if she wants to be involved with me in any capacity.

Further, I've even had a woman tell me she likes a man to play with her head. When I asked her what she meant, she told me she wanted me to make her think about my whereabouts. In other words, she wanted me to make her suspicious of another woman so she could feel like she had to work hard to keep me. Just in case you were wondering, I let her find someone who could accommodate her. Game time is over, folks.

We must change our attitude towards dating. Our children are suffering because of our ignorance. Let's take a leap of faith and rid our minds of the nonsense that's breaking down the family unit with no end in sight. And remember, a woman does not fit into the cracks of a man's life. Case closed.

THE IMPORTANCE OF RESEARCH

ALWAYS REMEMBER, WHENEVER any type of research is done, the sources by which the researcher obtains information must be considered. Not only are they to be considered, but the researcher must also assure the sources are reliable. The information obtained through the research process must come from individuals who are respected in their field of study, consistent with the views of others in that chosen field, and conclusively substantiated. Check out the accused's sources of information. Athletes, movie and television stars, ex-cons, hustlers, inmates, ministers and deacons—the very men women are complaining about. All his friends who would only tell him what they thought he wanted to hear.

Now, let's compare these characters to the standards listed above. They're not reliable, not at the top of their field, their opinions vary, and they can't conclusively substantiate their findings. In other words, what their testimony amounts to would be considered no more than hearsay testimony in a court of law. And so everyone is clear, hearsay testimony, as most of us know, isn't permissible within the judicial system, nor within God's court of law. One must have firsthand knowledge of the case in question. Since most of my opposing counsel's clients keep their Bibles in the back window of their cars, we can't rely on them for a firsthand account of the events in question. The most we can hope to get from them is what they heard from someone else. Therefore, they are barred from testifying in open court.

Take a look at the lead defendant's credentials in this case. He openly boasts about the many failed relationships he's had and believes, as a result of his many failed relationships, he has gained superior insight over God as to how one can successfully maintain a relationship, thereby nominating himself as the poster child for explaining the male mindset to women.

Once again, if you were to listen to him and not your mother's keen insight into a man's mind, you would have failed to use the one resource that will help you unlock the mysteries you've been so desperately waiting for. As the saying goes, "Mama knows best."

Unquestionably, what you have in this poor explanation of a man's mind is the mindset of a grown boy and a few grown boys who told him exactly what he wanted to hear. He clearly stated that he couldn't consider anything or anyone before he accomplished his goals—not even his own family was to be considered. This is exactly the way a boy thinks.

On the opposite end of the spectrum, a real man is able to balance both work and family no matter what his state of being may be. Before he goes to bed at night, he makes his plans as to how he will go about keeping his family together. Further, when a real man wakes up in the morning and his feet hit the floor, he looks at his family, grabs the bull by the horns, wrestles him to the ground, and begins his journey—never giving concern for himself or his station in life. Nothing or anybody will get in a real man's way of providing for his family. That's a real man.

The defendant's book claims to be the tell-all, self-help guide to all of women's problems with men. Without any stretch of the imagination, this book is a no-help guide for all fools who want to believe in it. It is absolutely, emphatically garbage—no humor intended.

The damage that black men have caused to our women's confidence in us appears to me to be insurmountable. This book only adds insult to injury. If we're going to turn the tide, we must begin now, and our steps must be large and courageous. We can began by trashing this no-help book and learning to hear the voice of a wise man versus that of a fool. Check out the comparison I have formulated for you below, so you will be able to recognize foolishness when you see it. And remember, a leopard never changes its spots.

Food For Thought: The difference between a wise man and a fool.

▸ A wise man speaks life. A fool speaks death.
▸ A wise man knows when to speak up. A fool doesn't know when to shut up.
▸ A wise man will tell you something that will add value to your life. A fool will tell you something that detracts value from your life.
▸ A wise man will tell you something that you can tell someone else, and they will think you're the smartest person in the world. A fool will tell you something, and as soon as you open your mouth, everyone will know you're a fool.
▸ When a wise man speaks, his mind keeps running. When a fool speaks, his mind shuts off, and his mouth keeps running like an automatic machine gun.

Note: If fools keep their mouths shut, no one will ever know they're fools. Stay tuned in as I continue to chip away at this debacle called a book.

COUNT 3

WHAT DRIVES BOYS

FROM THE OUTSET, I am not from the school of thought that believes a woman cannot raise a boy to be a man. After all, she is man-kind. In addition, my mother raised me, and she did a damn good job; that's why I won't accept the first thing that comes my way. However, I do believe it's important for a boy to be in a man's presence to teach him the few things a woman may not have experience with. These few things a woman may not be able to teach a boy, however, do not equal the totality of what constitutes a man.

Ladies, if you find yourself raising a young boy on your own, remember, it takes a village to raise a person. You're not alone. There are many places you can get help in the areas you're not comfortable with. There are many organizations that are genuinely concerned with assisting our young men with their transition into manhood. I am not talking about your deacon at the church who will want to lay hands on you as a reward for doing a humane act.

"Get this into your head . . ." "Once you've learned that . . ." Those were the defendant's exact words to women. Is he talking to women or children? These are the exact words I've heard parents use when they are disciplining their children. Only a boy wouldn't understand the gentleness with which a man speaks to his woman.

I now understand what the offender meant by manhood being a lifetime pursuit for some of us. He has perfectly described the DNA of a boy.

33

Who boys are—*I'm the man.* What they do—*I'm an NFL player.* What they make—*I just signed a million-dollar contract.* Don't be mistaken. This is the mentality of a boy.

A man is defined by his character. Not who he is, but whose is he? Not what he does, but does he take pride in what he does, no matter what it is? Not how much he makes, but what does he do with what he makes, and who benefits from it? Not where he lives, but does he know his own address when he finishes work? Not what kind of ring he has, but does he take off his wedding ring when he's away from his wife? And, finally, not how many children he has, but does he hide his children's pictures to conceal his true identity?

The "who we are, what we have, and where we're going" concept preached in Steve's book reminds me of the way a boy thinks. All these ingredients are needed to assure a boy's ego. No real man will measure his success based on materialism.

A real man's success can be determined by his family's reaction to him when he enters the house. Is his family happy to see him, or do they wish he never came home? Do his kids run to him or in the other direction? Does his wife greet him with a blessed kiss or continue what she's doing as if he never walked into the house? These are indicators of a man's success, not money.

In addition, one trying to escape the effects of slavery will also utilize these principals to validate one's worthiness. We have been robbed of our rich traditions and customs that placed family in the fore, that compelled a man to consider family first, always, when at the helm, charting a course for his family. Some of us have been westernized and now measure a man's success according to their standards. As a result, our men have a false concept of what constitutes a man and have found themselves caught in this web of deception, trying to prove their manhood by being able to financially provide for their families, even at the expense of performing the crab-in-the-barrel mentality.

Furthermore, some of the things stated by the woman's voice (aka Steve) as being things needed by a man to assure him of his manhood places women in a subservient and dependent role, rendering her helpless without the assistant of a man. This type of thinking and treatment that places a man as the breadwinner is ancient history. Too many women are the top breadwinners of the family for this to be alive today. It doesn't matter who brings the most bacon home, as long as there's some bacon to eat; a man's pride shouldn't be damaged. As a matter of fact, if my woman made more money than me, so be it—she did what she had to do to be in her position. And that's not a bad thing. If I want to be in my woman's position, I can ask her how she got there, and I can do the same thing. It's not about competition, people. It's about survival.

I believe the true strength of a man lies within his desire, willingness, and commitment to attend to one family and one family only. He's willing to stick it out and deal with the trails of a relationship regardless of his station in life.

A true man is vigilant to his family's needs and makes pain-staking efforts to see those needs are met. Nothing will deter him from keeping his family together. Come rain, hail, sleet, or snow, a real man will do what he must do to no end. A pack of wild horses couldn't drag him away from his responsibilities to his family—that includes remaining faithful to his wife. That's what real men do. Take a look at the comparison of a man versus a boy to see if you can identify your man's uniform.

MEN VERSUS BOYS

▸ A boy thinks with his head between his legs. A man thinks with his head on his shoulders.
▸ A boy buys his girlfriend flowers on Valentine's Day only. A man buys his lady flowers throughout the year.

- A boy will visit his girlfriend in the hospital when it's convenient for him. A man will spend every night at the hospital with his woman until she gets better.
- A boy will leach off of his girlfriend. A man will take care of his wife.
- A boy spends more time with his homeboys than he does with his family. A man will always make time for his family first. He enjoys spending time with his family over anything.
- A boy will give his girlfriend the beat-up car. A man will give his woman the luxury car.
- A boy will put himself first. A man will always take care of his woman's needs first.
- A boy's girlfriend must beg or demand things from him. A man will ask his woman if she's in need of anything. She doesn't have to demand.
- A boy will be embarrassed to go get his girlfriend's feminine needs from the store. A man will go with pride and never mumble a word.
- A boy will try to exert dominance. A man works in harmony with his woman.
- A boy snaps at everything with the appearance of offense to his family and is ready to kill someone. A man will evaluate the situation and work out a diplomatic solutions.
- A boy talks the talk but doesn't walk the walk. A man doesn't talk about what he will do; he does what he will do.
- A boy is king only in the bed. A man is king of his entire house.
- A man attends to his family needs. A boy is always in need.
- A man thrives off the challenge of caring for his family. A boy walks around with his tail curled up like a frightened dog.
- A boy plans only for himself. A man plans for his family, and then he thinks about himself.
- A man is resourceful in times of difficulty. A boy finds it difficult to be resourceful; he walks around like a chicken with its head chopped off.
- A man plans ahead. A boy has no plans at all.

▸ No matter how tough things get, a man never loses hope. A boy's hopes are dashed with the first sign of trouble.

Check Point: So, after reading that list, are you confident that your man is actually a man?

THE DRIVING FORCE of a man is his family. Not who he is, what he has, and where he's going. A real man understands the true meaning of love. He understands that when he expresses his love to his family it is a matter of the heart. What he does for his family is not to boast or prove anything to anyone. He provides for his family purely out of love. A true man also will never look for anything in return for doing that which God ordained him to do. Otherwise, his efforts are vain and done only to achieve some selfish desire to benefit him and him alone. Be advised, God searches our hearts as well in relation to our efforts towards him. He will go over our hearts with a fine-tooth comb and see the superficial reasons we make felonious claims of our love for him.

My sisters, I have thought about every civilization in the history of mankind to discover the driving force of a man. Conclusively, I have found a man's family to be unequivocally the reason for his existence. There is no other source of drive that comes close to that of a man's family. If you go over the comparison above and a preponderance of the evidence weighs in the direction of a boy beyond a shadow of doubt, you have a boy on your hands. Sex, things, and sex and things again—that's what drives boys.

COUNT 4

Boys Like to Hunt

I T APPEARS TO me that the theory of a man liking to hunt is founded on the fact that men have an aggressive nature and they enjoy the thrill of being the hunter and not the hunted. Don't forget, a woman is a man with a womb—Womb-Man. She is also a part of the Hu-Man-Race. In other words, Hu-Men-Kind (hyu-men-kind). She is just like a man. So, as one can see, just from this definition, we can't exclude the female from liking to hunt or fish. And some women do like to hunt and fish—even with respects to dating.

First, let's look at some familiar real life examples to refute this theory that men like to hunt. Then, we will ratify our position with scripture. Don't get mad; I know a lot of people spent money on the false doctrines of the unlearned. I'm only cleaning house. Besides, I've never been in a fair fight. There are no love affairs in war. We're going to Africa—the Motherland.

EXAMPLE #1
There have been many stories that have been told about vast numbers of African traditions. Books have been written and movies have been produced to enlighten us on the African culture. As a matter of our concern, it's one tradition prevalent to this book's position—that's a boy becoming a man.

According to this tradition, in order for a boy to prove his worthiness of transitioning into manhood, he must prove himself by conquering certain obstacles. The first one: a boy must be able to hunt in order to show he is capable of providing for a family. During this process, the clan leaders (the men) are back at the village relaxing with their honeys. They've already proven their manhood. In other words, their oats have already been sorted. They have nothing to prove.

The new men of the clan take the boys out on the expedition and evaluate their performance. During this expedition certain requirements must be met in order for the boy to achieve the desired outcome. For instance, the prey must be of a certain kind and size—a worthy opponent—and it must be performed alone in the face of death. If a boy fails to meet these requirements, his transition to manhood will be halted, and he will be forbidden to mingle with the men: a sacred place reserved only for those who have successfully sorted their oats. The boy failed to get the big one. He is not a man yet.

Once the boys seeking manhood have accomplished their task, the young men leading the expedition report back to the clan leaders. If the report is music to the clan leaders' ears, a celebration will be given in honor of the new men of the clan. At the celebration, the new men would be a prime target for a new sugar boo. The fathers of the clan would be excited about matching their daughters with the new men. The new men have proven they're capable of providing for a family, and therefore, they are ready to rock the boat—don't pass go and don't collect two hundred dollars. Turn out the lights, baby. I'm a true man. It's time to get my prize jewel. They hunt no more.

EXAMPLE #2

As we continue our journey through Africa, we recall that a lion is infamously known as the king of the jungle. He's the most feared creature in the jungle. From what I heard, he wasn't always that way. Somebody rubbed him the wrong way.

For those who don't know, lions exert their power in their early days. Once a lion establishes he is the man, he gets the pick of the liter and is respected by everyone in the clan. From that point on, he stays back at the house with his sweetie and waits for the boys to bring the bacon home. He's a man now. He hunts no more. He has nothing else to prove. He knows what he got beside him every night and he's proud. If you are still in doubt, just watch one of the animal shows. Boys hunt.

EXAMPLE #3

> *Now therefore take, I pray thee, thy weapons, thy quiver and thy bow, and go out to the field, and take me some venison. And make me savory meat, such as I love, and bring it to me, that I may eat; that my soul may bless thee before I die.*
>
> (GENESIS 27:3–4)

This passage of scripture is further proof of the false notion of a man liking to hunt. At some point in life, a man's desire and ability to hunt will cease. As this scripture illustrates, Isaac realized his hunting days were far behind him. He had nothing else to prove, and the thrill of hunting satisfied him no more. He was satisfied with his station in life and was prepared to pass the torch on to his man-child.

Word to the wise: If a boy doesn't capture his prey by a certain age, he will be looked upon with disrepute. He would leave the village as a result of the shame of not being considered a man. He is considered a boy for eternity. He will be looked upon by all who know him as a disgrace to his people. No father will want to place his daughter in the hands of a weak man.

We should employ the same standards with respect to our own lives today. So, ladies, if you're dealing with someone who can't wait a couple of weeks until you get in the mood, you have a boy on your hands, who will never transition into manhood. He has failed to catch the big one, condemning himself to boyhood forever. It isn't going to happen—no way, Jose.

I've given several excellent examples above to refute the idiopathic theology of the so-called relationship expert on his theory of a man liking to hunt. By now, I know my readers realize the fallacies presented to you in the defendant's book, and you're ready to throw it in the trash. Don't do it. I'm not finished. Besides, I'm going to need something to get my fireplace started next winter. Better yet, take it back to the bookstore and ask for a refund. If they don't refund your money, sue the writer for fraud on the basis of misrepresenting himself as a relationship expert. I'll testify on your behalf.

Now, come and follow me back to the garden one more time. *"And the rib, which the Lord God had taken from man, made he a woman, and [brought] her unto the man"* (Genesis 2:22). As one can see from this scripture, Adam wasn't looking for a woman. Eve was presented to him. In other words, a man doesn't have to be on a hunt to find a wife.

For further proof, look at Proverbs 18:22, the famously quoted scripture with regard to a man finding a wife. This passage of scripture has been misappropriated within the church for years. It is taught that a man is the one to be on a hunt if he is to find a wife. The lady should just sit back and wait for her knight to come ridding in on his white horse and knock on her front door. Negative. God will set the situation up if we just be patient. Hold on, my people, your mule is coming.

Now, check this out. Remember that money you found you weren't looking for—you switched back to another purse and found some money or you put on a jacket and found some money you didn't know you had or you took some clothes to the cleaners and the cleaner presented you with some money you left in a pocket. As one can see, a man doesn't have to be on a hunt to find a wife.

If we sit back, relax, and enjoy the ride, God will present a wife to us. Without fail, He will choose a perfect match for us. God's method of matchmaking has been working since the beginning of time. His batting average is one hundred percent, and it will never be outdone. What God puts together, stays together.

"What therefore God hath joined together, let no man put asunder" (Mark 10:9). If God truly joined it together, no man can, will, or dare try to separate it.

I firmly believe in the art of presentation. As the saying goes, "the first impression is a lasting impression." Somewhere along the line, the guidelines of presentation have been distorted, causing too many people to seek unworthy methods of presentation in attempt to replace the real thing. As a result, many people focus on the superficial aspects of a relationship rather than the aspects of inner-beauty. My house, car, breast, and booty—just to name a few.

Furthermore, to even refer to the process of obtaining a mate as a game is catastrophic in itself. God's business of matching people together is serious business and should be taken as such. It's not a game. He frowns on those who make a mockery of his institutions, and there are serious consequences for doing such, up to and including (spiritual) death.

ADDICTIVE PERSONALITY

THE IDEOLOGY OF pursuing a relationship as a game is much like a drug addict pursuing his/her next fix. They are constantly looking for that same feeling as the first—the big one, the one that will satisfy their adrenaline rush, the instant gratification.

The sin of lust works very much the same way. A lust addict is never satisfied. The more we do it, the more we want it. Be advised, an addict will stop at nothing to get what he/she wants. They will go as far as to curse God if He gets in the way. I'm talking from experience—not what someone told me.

Until an addict is confronted with reality, they will continue to abuse their body to no end. Amazingly, an addict will reason with themselves that everyone is wrong, and not them—they don't have a problem.

Unfortunately for those around an addict, the addict will never get the help they desperately need until they stop fooling themselves. Take a leap of faith.

As a result of continued abuse, our system will grow a tolerance for lust, and we will become too blind to see the devastating situation we're in. We will search high and low looking for a dealer who we think has what we want. We size up the dealer, we look at how the product is packaged, and we take a little test before we put it in us—test the waters first. And, based on our superficial method of determining its value, we overdose and must be taken to the hospital for emergency care.

In reality, it is my belief there's only one pusher who can supply all our needs. He has never failed, He has never lost a patient, He has never lost a court case, and He keeps stellar records. *"But my God shall supply all my need according to his riches in glory by Christ Jesus"* (Philippians 4:19).

We cannot rely on someone's advice whose life and resources are flawed. Finding a mate is too important to be trusted to someone who will tell you what they think you want to hear. If we would dip our nose in God's word more than once in a while, we will get the blueprint for finding a mate.

To promote God in one breath and promote sexual immorality in another breath is hypocritical and should be shunned at all cost.

God has established a specific model for obtaining a mate that must be adhered to with no variations. Any variations to God's model are futile and a waste of one's time.

> *No man can serve two masters: for either he will hate the one, and love the other; or else he will hold to the one, and despise the other. Ye cannot serve God and mammon.*
>
> (MATTHEW 6:24)

In other words, you cannot straddle the fence. One must make a decision as to whom they will give allegiance to: sex or love. And believe me, sex and love don't see eye to eye.

In addition, giving false testimony is against God's laws as well as man's laws. In both cases, severe punishment is handed down. In biblical days, these offenses could result in one being beheaded, and anyone caught reading their books will have the same thing done to them. You can take that to the bank and cash it.

It is my honest belief that the accused I'm prosecuting was talking about finding a girlfriend: something to play with, a booty call, hit or miss, when it's convenient. Do you really want to be someone's girlfriend or plaything for the rest of your life?

My sisters, hunting is child's play. Once a man has captured his prey, his hunting days are over. He now turns his attention to securing his prey and taking it home for keeps: it's his and his alone. He has what he wants, and no one dare try to take it away. He will guard, cultivate, and take care of his captured with every fiber of his being. It's his life source, and he will cherish it and do whatever it takes to keep it. And everyone around him will know he loves his wife by the way he gives detailed attention to her in season and out of season. Actions speak louder than words. Boys hunt, not men. The end!

THERE'S NO EXCUSE FOR CHEATING

True love brings you home every night.

Note: *Ignorantia juris non excusat*—Ignorance of the law does not excuse.

As I continue the journey through this case, it's clear to me the defendant is suffering from a serious identity crisis when it relates to God, love, and sex. He occasionally makes reference to God's name, but there's no evidence that he would know God if He walked up on him and slapped him in the face. Hell, Satan knows God's name.

It's extremely troubling to the prosecution to see such disregard for the ordinances God has established even before the foundations of the earth. To promote cheating is contradictory to God's standards and should be eschewed without consideration for one's feelings.

During this discourse, keep in mind, when I make reference to cheating, I'm specifically talking about cheating with regard to a husband and a wife. I'm not talking about a girlfriend–boyfriend situation or a man and a woman cheating on one another. Why?

Because if a man and a woman are not married, they have no obligation to be loyal to each other—obligation only comes before the presence of God when two people say "I do." Hence, girlfriend and boyfriend, you are excluded from this conversation. If you don't believe me, look at the next two examples:

EXAMPLE #1

If you and your man were in a car accident, and an emergency procedure needed to be done, and he couldn't make a decision, they would come to you and ask you if you were his next of kin. If you were to tell the doctor you are not his next of kin, the doctor would say: "Well, who is?"

After discovering you're not the next of kin, the doctor will prevent you from making a decision on his life. Reason being, you're not his wife—nor are you considered his family. There are no entitlement benefits issued out at the hospital. The hospital will not be sued by you presenting them with a fake ID. Girlfriends, you are not the wife. Forget about it. I don't care how long you've been dropping it like it's hot. It isn't going to happen.

EXAMPLE #2

You've been with a man for the last twenty years and he dies. You've been playing house, but he never married you. Everything is in his name: the house, cars, and he has a separate bank account from yours. Little do you know, he never divorced his wife. . . . You think you are set up well and everything is going to be okay. Think again, because you are in for a rude awakening. His wife will get everything. The house, the cars, the money in the bank, and the insurance policy money. You will get absolutely nothing. You will be left standing there looking like a deer caught in the headlights of a car.

Taking it a little deeper, some of his family members won't even acknowledge you as his spouse at the funeral. His wife will be sitting with the family, and you will be sitting in the back looking as silly as a peacock eating a bowl of chili. I'm sorry, my sister, but the truth is what it is. Girlfriends are excluded. So, pack your bags, get on the bus, or take a hike. You are about to be uprooted.

We cannot change the rules to God's game to our benefit and expect to get the same benefits of married couples. I have never read anything in the Bible about playing house. This is man's doing and has nothing to do with God. One can use any excuse they want to, but your makeshift relationship will not be accepted in God's eyes. I know this sounds weird to a lot of people, but it's God's way or the highway.

Let's look at this from a different angle. When two unmarried people engage in an affair of their do-it-yourself relationship, both of them are actually cheating on God. God is the Father, and He has not given the bride away—both male and female. Therefore, your relationship is faulty from the outset, and the parties participating in the act commit spiritual adultery against God. You can't mix mud and water in a glass and expect the end result to be drinkable. It's like that, and that's the way it is.

AGRICULTURE ASSESSMENT

WHEN WE LOOK at why men cheat from the prospective of the opposing book, let's take a hard look at cheating with regard to aeration, its origin, and its beginning. In other words, we must look at where cheating starts, how cheating is cultivated, and what brings cheating to life.

I have selected an agriculture analogy similar to that of the parable of the sower in order to attempt to make it as plain as possible for my readers. From this analogy, one should be able to easily conclude why men cheat, and how they can go home, get in the bed, and look their unsuspecting wife in the face as if nothing happened—I've just described a trifling dog. The evidence presented will be so obvious an excuse for cheating will be made void of one's vocabulary.

First, let's explore the aeration approach to cheating. Aeration is the practice of creating holes in the ground (which, in this analogy, represents the mind) to allow seeds to be impregnated into the soil deep enough to be fertilized and begin the process of growing into life. The aeration technique can be tedious, and it must be done over a period of time. Moreover, the measures taken during this process must be planned and strategically carried out to achieve the desired results.

With men, here's how the aeration process starts: Typically, but not always, a father sets the stage for his son's mind to be aerated. The boy is allowed to watch television programs with a high content of sex, discovers his dad's collection of porn videos and nude magazines, sees his dad flirting with women other than his mother—and sadly, the boy is encouraged by his dad to rob an unsuspecting young woman of her virginity. Hence, aeration—the tilling of the ground. A perfect environment for a future cheater.

It is extremely important that one remembers this process. Why? Satan and his demon's abilities are limited. They are incapable of performing the aeration process. Therefore, in order for their tricks to work one must help them make an opening for their devices to take root. Otherwise, their efforts to gain access will be futile, and you will be protected. No hurt, harm, or danger will make its way to your front door.

Caution: Don't let your mind be impregnated with the wiles of the devil. Put on the Helmet of Salvation and protect your thoughts. This is not a cliché. A helmet is a part of the uniform of any soldier, no matter what type of war is being fought.

Continuing: Once the aeration of a boy's mind is completed, we must look at cheating from its origin—where it all began. The seeds planted by the father in the fallopian tube (the boy's mind) begin to fuse with the ovum (the boy's hormones).

Then, it is nourished in the fertile, untainted soil of the womb (the boy's heart) to create new life form, an invasive species that accelerates at an alarming rate. The boy starts noticing changes down low, he begins to date, the memory of his dad's porn videos and nude magazines are a reality now, and those half-naked women he saw on television he can now see live and up close everywhere he goes. He can't evade those early images. They haunt him both day and night. Everywhere he goes he notices breast and booty. On the streets, in his school, at his auntie's house, and, yes, even in the church—that's all he can think about. He thinks about it every time he sees a female: his teacher, his doctor, and his homeboy's sister. If the wind blows the wrong way, he will think about it. The seed of lust has been successfully planted and has taken root—its origin.

This seed is planted so deep in him that once it sprouts, the slightest change in atmosphere will cause him to kick violently from within. The spasms will come every five minutes. If he smells perfume, it will be like a Fourth of July fireworks show. And, like most boys, after wrestling with these emotions for so long, nothing or anybody will get in his way of this newfound manhood as it seizes the boy's mind and body. Not surprising, however, his daddy will be there cheering him on every step of the way. This leads us into the final phase of the cheating process. It's time for the baby to be born.

Finally, the birth or the beginning of cheating: The boy, in spite of all the other people who informed him that having sex outside the ordinance of God is wrong, still begins his quest to give birth to the child raging inside of him. His pastor told him it wasn't right, his uncle who is faithful to his wife told him it wasn't right, and even his homeboy's dad who is faithful to his wife told him it wasn't right. But against all godly wisdom, he still decides to give birth to something that can destroy something more precious than his three minutes of fame. He searches high and low until he finds a victim, and before he knows it, it's over and both of them are left wondering, "Was it really worth it?" There's no excuse for cheating.

Since the beginning of humanity, God has given man the ability to choose between right and wrong. And in doing so, He has ensured everyone is made aware of the differences between the two extremes. As a result, there will be no saying, "I didn't know what I was doing." There's no such thing as happenstance—or, it just happened. Saying you were drunk doesn't work either. Neither will your age be a good defense. We may be able to lie to one another and justify within ourselves that cheating is okay, but it won't work with God—I'm one hundred percent sure of that.

The reasons stated by the defendant for cheating are frivolous and trumped-up excuses for a man doing what he really wants to do. There's absolutely nothing a woman can do to cause a man to cheat. This is a psychology used by king manipulators to justify their lustful desires. They hope, by providing what they believe to be a valid reason for cheating, they will be able to have their cake and eat it too—don't fall for that mess, sisters.

The excuse-for-cheating philosophy is really nothing but the blame game. The object of this game is to get one to believe they're responsible for someone else's actions. The cheater will even go as far as to make the other party feel guilt for their cheating. They will say things like: *you didn't do this or that; you made me do it; you wouldn't give me any; and you know a man got to have it.* And we all know from the woman's voice that's what boys do.

Be aware, it's much easier to blame someone else for your shortcomings than to accept responsibility for your own actions. If you're a cheater, don't punk out, be a man, and accept responsibility for who you are—be all you can be. And God knows, please don't say your homeboy made you do it. He wasn't there pulling the trigger for you.

Face it, the birth of your new child is illegitimate, and God is not pleased at all. There are no disclaimers to his laws. Grace doesn't excuse us from the act of sin. Grace only excuses a believer from eternal spiritual damnation. No excuse you give to God for cheating will be acceptable. So don't waste your time. When you get to the pearly gates, just throw yourself upon the mercy of the court. As your attorney, that's the best advice I can give you.

A SERMON I HEARD

T HE REASONS STATED for cheating by the opposing counsel reminds me of a sermon I heard recently, titled "THE WRONG DIRECTION." The preacher's central theme was this: What does one do when they get there? THERE! Meaning, after we have reached a certain accomplishment (e.g., got the woman we want), what causes us to go in the wrong direction? What prevents us from evaluating our position and keeps us from enhancing that which we already have? In our case, he's talking about cultivating your own home.

The character used by this preacher to explain this dilemma was King Herod Agrippa II. Briefly, this king comes from a line of kings infamously known as killers. Herod Agrippa II's grandfather is notoriously known as the king who got upset at the birth of Jesus and tried to have him killed. Simple enough.

In a futile attempt to validate his position, this preacher cited three theories to illustrate why he believed Herod followed the murderous customs of his Herodian forefathers: the sociology theory, the biology theory, and the affirmation theory. I was not convinced. Here's why: I study and I don't take any man's word for face value. I don't care what title a man has behind his name; he's not intelligent enough to interpret the scriptures for me—that's the responsibility of the Holy Spirit.

THEORY BLUNDERS

#1 THE SOCIOLOGY THEORY:

According to this theory, one makes decisions based on their environmental upbringing—what type of parents they have, their acquaintances, religious background, education, etc. The congregation was attentive, studious, and appeared to be very excited about what the preacher was saying during this sermon. For me, at first glance, this theory resonated well until searched out. Once my brain kicked in and I began to analyze this theory in regard to Adam, I had no choice but to disagree. I will state my reason for rejecting this theory in the refutation section shortly.

#2 THE BIOLOGY THEORY:

According to this theory, one makes decisions based on their genetics—the genes received from their parents. Meaning, since Herod II's parents were killers, he had no choice but to follow in their footsteps. In other words, Herod's parent's genetics were responsible for his actions. Once again, I disagreed.

#3 The Affirmation Theory:

According to this theory, we do things seeking the approval of those we view as important to us—similar to what is known in the military as a spotlight Ranger. We seek to please our family, our boss, our friends, our pastor, and anyone we deem important. We seek their approval, believing it will put us in high regards with them. I disagree.

Now, children, put your thinking caps on. The woman's voice has based a tremendous amount of his reasoning in his entire book on the aforementioned theories. At this time, I will revisit the Garden of Eden to dispel each of these theories with ease and simplicity.

#1 Sociology Theory Refutation:

> *And the Lord God planted a garden eastward in Eden; and there he put the man whom he had formed.*
>
> (Genesis 2:8)

The Garden of Eden is referred to as a place of paradise, delight, fruitfulness, and enjoyment. Adam and Eve had everything they needed. They had eternal bliss, the best of the best, good friends, and the best rearing possible. They were even given the authority to name their playmates. Moreover, they wanted nor lacked anything. Therefore, if we conclude that Adam and Eve sinned because of their sociological orientation, we accuse God of being an unfit father and connect him with sin. We accused God of providing an atmosphere not sociologically conducive for His children. That's something I'm not willing to do. People, the saying is true: "A mind is a terrible thing to waste."

#2 BIOLOGY THEORY REFUTATION:

> *So God created man in his own image, in the image of God created he him; male and female created he them.*
>
> (GENESIS 1:27)

As you can see, even this theory doesn't work well. Adam and Eve were created in the image of God. That means they had extraordinary genes—their DNA was perfect. And we all know there's no fault in God. They had all the attributes of God except: *"I am that I am."* They had love, compassion, and wisdom, just to name a few.

#3 AFFIRMATION THEORY REFUTATION:

> *And God said, Let us make man in our image, after our likeness: and let them have dominion over....*
>
> (GENESIS 1:26)

As one can see, Adam had control of everything. He was the supreme authority here on earth—the HNIC. He had nothing to prove to anyone—he was the man. Everything and everybody looked up to him. Nothing was supposed to take place without his permission. Everything was to come through him. He had no one to answer to but God. So why and who would he need affirmation from? Theory rejected.

Though faulty, each one of these theories were presented with great charisma and an air of profoundness. Nevertheless, as one can see, it is extremely important not to get too emotional when listening to someone speak on what is supposed to be God's word or the rule of law. Jumping up and down and speaking in tongues has its place. However, when it comes to knowing the truth, one's mind must be able to determine the validity of the speaker's words. This can only come from a careful study of the Holy Scriptures.

If you don't remember anything else, remember this one thing: Speaking on God's word isn't like giving a stock forecast. When the stock market crashes, investors lose their money. On the contrary, when God's word is slanted, people may lose their life and soul; and the life I am talking about may be yours. Be diligent and search the scriptures. I guarantee you God will guide you to the truth.

Note: Excuses for cheating are like . . . everyone has one.

To my surprise, in his effort to give an excuse for doing wrong, this pastor also displayed the same reasoning most people use when it comes to the Old and New Testaments of the Bible, thereby giving the impression one need not even attempt to comply with the Old Testament. Case point, since we're in the dispensation of grace, there's no need to follow the Old Testament teaching, because they're obsolete and there is no way we can comply with the laws of the Old Testament. In other words, we don't have to worry about cheating, because we're going to cheat; it's just a matter of when. Besides, no need to worry, God's grace is a convenience store, and we can order forgiveness when we get ready. Following are a few scriptures frequently used as amendments to God's constitution:

THE AMENDMENTS TO THE CONSTITUTION OF GOD

DISCLAIMER SCRIPTURES

1) For all have sinned, and come short of the glory of God

(ROMANS 3:23).

2) For God so loved the world, that he gave his only begotten Son, that whosoever believeth in him should not perish, but have everlasting life

(JOHN 3:16).

F AR TOO OFTEN I have seen these passages and many more used in a manner that would lead one to believe they have a disclaimer to fall back on when they fail to upkeep God's laws. Sadly, this ideology typically is manifested from the pulpit. Preachers not well schooled in their craft misappropriate the scriptures and give the appearance they're issuing a license to sin. As a result, many comprehend these scriptures to mean, since we all have sinned and come short of the mark, what's the use? We may as well go ahead and sin and get it over with. And if you do, don't worry, we are saved by grace, can sin over and over again, and will be forgiven. We can become habitual sinners and don't have to worry about it. All we need to do is go to Cheaters Anonymous on Sundays, and everything will be all right.

CHEATERS ANONYMOUS FOR THE UNFAITHFUL

PROTOCOL:

- Welcome. My name is _____ and I'm a cheater-aholic.
- Here at Cheaters Anonymous, we make every excuse we can for cheating.
- We blame our wives for our cheating, and there was nothing we could've done to stop it—we're not the blame. Cheating is what we do, and that's just the way it is.
- Here at Cheaters Anonymous, we understand that if our wife doesn't feel like it, it's okay to get some from our sidepiece.
- We understand that making amends with our wives may be impossible—heck, we don't care. 'Cause we're the men. She can take it or leave it.

THE FINE PRINT

BUYER BEWARE

WHEN ONE ENTERS into a contract, it is extremely important to remember to read the fine print. If not, one can miss a vital piece of information that can be costly. In addition, having failed to read the entire contract, and by signing one's name, one will have no recourse and will be bound by the terms of the contract. Take a look at the fine print of God's contract that prevents us from thinking we have a license to sin.

GOD'S CONTRACT

What shall we say then? Shall we continue in sin, that grace may abound? Watch this! God forbid....

(ROMANS 6:1–2)

AS ONE CAN see from this passage, an excuse for cheating will not be admissible in God's court as a defense for committing spiritual crimes. Once again, being saved by grace only exempts us from eternal spiritual damnation (i.e., being eternally separated from God). We will still have to give an account for our wrongdoings on the Day of Judgment. *"Who will render to every man according to his deeds"* (Romans 2:6).

A CRIMINAL EXAMPLE

IT HAS BEEN my experience that people who get arrested and turn their lives around go to court thinking if they tell the judge they gave their life to Christ, they will escape the penalty of their crimes. To their surprise, the judge is happy they have changed their lives, but he informs them they must still give an account for their crimes—it works the same way with sin. We will give an account for everything we have done on this earth. So don't think you have an emergency escape plan from the Day of Judgment. There will be no get-out-of-jail free cards issued.

It is important to remember, when it comes to God and our cheating, it is a matter of the heart that is important. Yes, we're forgiven, but are we sorry for what we did, will we stop the lustful desires of our hearts, or will we go on a cheating spree just because we know we're forgiven? I don't think so. It doesn't work like that.

I would be the first to admit that living a life free from cheating is difficult. However, just because we're the benefactors of the aforementioned scriptures, we shouldn't perpetually indulge in cheating activities so grace can continue to show its face up. To do so is clear evidence of one who is abusing the system and demonstrating their heart is far from God. This would be considered an abuse of power and a lack of regard for the one who issued the power.

No one can deny the validity of the above scriptures. However, in the midst of this truth, one is not condemned for making an earnest attempt to at the very least comply with the laws of God. Otherwise, if a conscious effort is not made to adhere to God's laws, it is highly likely one may become a habitual cheater and develop total blindness to being faithful. As I stated earlier, a lot of people think we should do away with the Old Testament. But look at a simple explanation as to what Jesus had to say:

> *The Old Testament is the prophecy of things to come. I didn't come here to destroy it. If I do, I'm only going to be destroying myself. The laws of times past are just as valid today as they were yesterday. They may have been etched on stones yesterday, but they must be written on man's heart today.*

On the other hand, the New Testament is the fulfilling of things to come—I'm here. Therefore, the prophecy and the prophets have been fulfilled. So, I'm basically just backing up the law and the prophets. The law stands and even I can't change it.

These two books go hand in hand, and the New Testament is a sequel to the Old Testament. It is imperative for one to have an understanding of both books to get a complete picture of its entire message. Following are a few questions to motivate one to at least make an attempt to become a student of the Bible.

MOTIVATIONAL QUESTIONS

1. If you purchased a book by your favorite author, would you start reading in the middle of the book? No, you wouldn't. Well, that's exactly what we do when it comes to the Bible. We go straight to the New Testament, never giving any consideration to the rich history that lies between the pages of the Old Testament. I'm reminded of a saying: "If you don't know where you came from, how can you know where you're going?"

2. Why do we give more credence to a book that will add little, if any, value to our lives over the word manifested in the flesh? Answer: The book makes us feel good. The word pulls the covers off of us and shows us for what we really are—the truth hurts. The Bible is a mirror none of us want to stand in front of.

Cheating is a choice. There's nothing anyone can say to the contrary. As I stated earlier, an excuse for cheating is a sad attempt to justify a wrongdoing. Just in case you didn't hear me when I made the call in the section entitled "Boys Like to Hunt," allow me to send out another trumpet call referencing another analogy of a drug addict versus a cheater-filled lust addict. These two mentalities are like twins joined at the hip. They are like Manny, Moe, and Jack. They reason within themselves to continue in their addiction.

The lust that causes one to cheat functions much the same way as a drug to an addict. They are used to fulfill an excessive desire for the instantaneous gratification that these substances may bring.

Like a drug, cheating is a foreign substance to the constitution of the body and works contrary to the organisms within—it doesn't belong there. When digested, immediately certain changes take place between the internal parts that causes a violent reaction. Guilt, shame, disappointment, worthlessness, failure, heartache, and a troubled mind eat at the internal parts of a cheater—at least those who still have a tolerance to wrongdoing.

In the beginning these feelings can be strong and, in some cases, overpowering. However, if one continues on this path of self-destruction, these feelings slowly subside, and a tolerance for these foreign substances increases. As a result of this increased tolerance, the individual's system that is digesting these substances will ultimately become immune and require more and more to achieve the same effect. This is exactly how it works with the drug of cheating.

Notice, in the beginning, a cheater starts cheating by being an occasional user—they dip and dab every now and again. Next, they become a weekend user—they only cheat on the weekends when they can get away. As the addiction progresses, they cheat during the week until they finally become a full-blown cheater.

Be aware, once a full-blown cheater, a cheating addict will search high and low trying to find their next fix. They will get their fix by any means necessary. It doesn't matter where they get it from. It could be your best friend, sister, bridesmaid, your child, or a prostitute—nothing will get in the way of fulfilling the lustful desires of a cheater. A cheater will even lay down in the bed next to a snake to get its jollies off. Sadly, not even

God will keep them from getting their fix. They will attempt to reason with God and misquote a scripture trying to get Him to agree to curve the cheating rules.

THE ANSWER TO YOUR QUESTION

I KNOW SOME OF you have been wondering how your man could cheat on you. You're intelligent, beautiful, caring, and there's nothing you wouldn't do for your man and kids. Here is your answer: He is an addict. It has nothing to do with you. So stop blaming yourself for someone else's shortcomings. It's all about the choices he makes—free yourself from the guilt of thinking it is something you have done wrong. You are blameless.

Now, to help you recognize a cheater, see if any of the following statements sound familiar:

CHEATERS' SIGNATURE STATEMENTS

1. I can't live without it.
2. I got to have it.
3. I can stop anytime I want to.
4. If she doesn't give it to me, I will go somewhere else.
5. There's always a woman who is willing.
6. She will understand; if she doesn't, to hell with her.
7. I only cheated because I couldn't get any from you.
8. I am only a weekend cheater.
9. I only cheat when I'm away working.
10. I only did it just that one time.
11. It just happened.

12. I'm only a casual cheater.

13. The devil made me do it.

Note: Now ask yourself this: Where did you here this from? If any of the above statements sound familiar to you, you have a cheating addict on your hands. Don't be naïve and fooled by the fancy talk. Excuses! Excuses! Excuses! That's all they are.

Now, let the truth be told. What most call cheating really isn't cheating at all. The only way one can cheat outside of marriage is to cheat on God (Spiritual Adultery). As I stated earlier, unmarried couples are under no obligation to remain faithful to one another. It doesn't matter if a commitment was made to one another or not.

However, unmarried couples who cheat violate God's laws and violate the cheating clause to His contract. We were sequestered and bound by an oath to keep his commandments. Therefore, when a party to a contract violates a clause of the contract, the non-violating party is under no obligation to fulfill the rest of the contract. Thank God for his grace and mercy.

Two Ways of Cheating

Married Couples Cheating:

When someone who is married steps outside of their marriage, they double cheat—they cheat on God and their spouse. That is, of course, if God truly joined them together.

First, if married according to God's standards, when a party to a marriage contract steps outside their marriage, they violate their vows they made to one another. They took an oath with their hand placed over their heart before God and man to a life of fidelity. At least that was the intention.

Both parties entered into the contract with the hopes of a faithful and everlasting marriage. No one forced them or held a gun to their head making them get married. It is a contract they entered into freely and of their own will. The man stood at the altar glowing as his beautiful bride strolled down the aisle to his awaiting arms. And finally, the announcement: I NOW PRONOUNCE YOU HUSBAND AND WIFE. I hope you all noticed I didn't say: I UNITE THEE IN HOLY MATRIMONY. There's a reason for that. Can you figure it out?

Unfortunately, as a result of one side cheating (not always, but usually the man), they've marred the first and greatest institution created by God, and all hell breaks out. Often, as demonstrated earlier, the cheater will try to come up with every excuse imaginable. There is none!

Secondly, when married couples cheat, they cheat against God when they commit this atrocity. A marriage sometimes is a union between God and those who are uniting in matrimony. God is the third party to a Holy contract, and He has more interest invested in this union than the other parties. The whole world is watching—including Satan and his demons.

Further, future generations of people may base their decision on the institution of marriage according to how people perform in marriage before them. Some may refuse to get married because of the failure rate of marriages presented to them.

This double-dip cheating is traumatic to God and can result in a curse being placed on the perpetrator of this violent act. It breaks God's heart and causes tears to stream from His heart.

Unmarried Couples Cheating:

When two people have pre-marital sex with one another, they are actually cheating against God and not one another. Since the father is the one to give the bride away, having sex violates God's right and his authority to do so. He is the one who sets the policies and procedures for getting married—it is His jurisdiction and His alone. Be careful, we cannot under any circumstances change God's rules and make them null and void. We absolutely do not have that authority.

The Bible tells me God loves a sweet smelling savor. Therefore, when the stench of sin from a stench-filled wedding ascends to the heavens, God and the heavenly host must turn their back to keep from falling out from the smell—just like we do when a drunkard comes to church with a reeking smell. God must close the windows of heaven to keep the stench out and drown out the cheers coming from hell by Satan and his demons.

NEWS BULLETIN

Some of us think because we're getting married in a church, God is pleased with our showing up. Wrong! God was not given the opportunity to make preparations for the wedding and invite His honored guest. Instead, we took measures into our own hands and invited the scum of the earth to give us away—Satan. Satan gladly walked down the aisle with the bride as his demons posted up all throughout the church. The scum records the entire incident, sends a copy to God, and post notices on social media for all to see. God in turn is accused of being an unfit father and is made the laughingstock by His enemy.

This act is devastating to God's heart and causes him to turn his back on some of his beloved children. Leaving them to learn the hard way; God's children are left at the altar to party with the devil just like Job's children. Consequently, this lustful desire prevents one from hooking up with the soul mate God had for us. And believe me, when God said one, he meant exactly what he said. There is no such thing as over and over again until we finally get it right. We only get one shot at our soul mate. Face it, people—I have.

ALL MEN CHEAT

I HAVE HEARD COUNTLESS times women say all men cheat—not so. That is an absolute fallacy. Now, we must remember, when God created everything, He created two of each: that includes female dogs.

My sisters, just because you were cheated on countless times by the many different men you've had does not mean your girlfriend's husband is cheating on her. There are truly some faithful husbands in this world, and they don't deserve to be categorized in the cesspool of the unfaithful.

As a matter of fact, to set the record straight and dispel this fable, not only am I proof that all men don't cheat, but I have several friends who are faithful to their wives—at least when we refer to cheating from a carnal perspective. So check out my two cents and see what you think.

My Two Cents

DURING MY FIVE year marriage to my ex-wife, I never cheated on her. I had every opportunity to cheat if I wanted. For example, within the course of our marriage, we separated three times in six-month increments. However, I honored God in our marriage even though these recent revelations from God about marriage were unknown to me at the time. When I said "I do," I really meant it.

Sadly, as soon as some of her so-called girlfriends found out we were separated, they were glad to accommodate me with cheating. I was not surprised.

However, it always baffled me how someone could mess with someone while they are with another and then turn around and expect them to be faithful to them when they get them. Help me out here because I might be a little crazy, but you all let me know if this next statement is true: Ladies, be advised, if a cheater cheats with you, they will cheat against you and give you the same medicine. A leopard doesn't change its spots.

People, once again, cheating is a choice. So, if you are a dog, don't deny it. Be the best dog you can be. But while you're being a dog, don't involve innocent people in your mess. If cheating is what you do, just don't get married.

THE CHEATER'S TOLERANCE TEST

WWYD

1. If your spouse cheated on you, what would you do?
   a. Would you leave them?
   b. Could you forgive them?
   c. Would you ever have trust in them again?
   d. Could you forget about what they've done to you?
   e. Would you be able to live in harmony with them?

2. If you cheated on your spouse, what would you want them to do?
   a. Would you want them to forgive you?
   b. Would you expect them to stay with you?
   c. Do you think they would ever be able to trust you again?
   d. Do you think they would be able to live in harmony with you?
   e. Do you think they could forget about what you did to them?

MY RESPONSE

BE ADVISED, MY two cents on these questions is in no way, shape, or form meant to be construed as advice. It is only what works for me. I can't live anyone's life for them.

There is no way I could invoke in my mind the possibility of my staying with someone who cheated on me. I understand everyone deserves a second chance—we all make mistakes. However, cheating violates the trust clause in a relationship, and I just can't see getting by it. As I stated earlier, cheating is no mistake; it's a choice. It is the straw that breaks the camel's back as far as I'm concerned. Trust is the engine that makes a relationship go, and without it, your engine will blow, causing your relationship to stop in its tracks. The good memories of your relationship will disappear in the blink of an eye.

Now, my sisters, stop using these shade-tree relationship experts for resolving your issues—especially those who allege it is okay for a man to cheat on his spouse. Consult the true expert and you will never go wrong. Next, I want you to answer a couple more simple questions.

COMMON SENSE ANALYSIS

---

1. Would you take your brand-spanking-new BMW to a jackleg mechanic? No, you wouldn't.

2. Would you take your fancy Porsche to a Ford dealership to get it fixed? No, you wouldn't.

3. Would you let your cousin June Bug go under your hood? No, you wouldn't. He'd steal your parts and try to sell them back to you.

4. Would you bet your money on One-Leg Uncle Willie in a footrace? No, you wouldn't.

SO, WHY ARE you entrusting your mind, body, and soul to someone who clearly doesn't give a damn about you. Furthermore, while there're working on you, they're sitting under the shade tree with their boys sipping on 40s, smoking blunts, losing parts to your engine, trying to figure out how they can be your permanent mechanic with benefits, and can't find their tools. That's just the kind of mechanic I would let work on my car—just so I can be pissed off and ask for a refund. Stop! Stop! Stop!

MAKE A U-TURN

ANY OF US have this false impression as to what it means to have it going on. We think because we have a big house, nice car, money in the bank, and all the women we want—we're blessed among the best. We can do whatever we want, and that's okay. Sorry, not so. God is not pleased and you shouldn't be either.

> *Unto the angel of the church of Ephesus write; These things saith he that holdeth the seven stars in his right hand, who walketh in the midst of the seven golden candlesticks. I know thy works, and thy labor ... Nevertheless, I have somewhat against thee, because thou hast left thy first love.*
>
> (REVELATIONS 2:1–4)

Here's what the Lord is saying: I see your worldly successes— the nice cars and house you have—and the beautiful wife I blessed you with that you're cheating on. Nevertheless, all that *shigady* don't mean a hill of beans to me. You're doing all that to impress the world, not Christ. You started out good—speaking in tongues, quoting scriptures to everybody, wearing your cross everywhere you went, holding your wife hand everywhere you went, testifying in church about how God blessed you with a good thing. Now, the pastor doesn't even know you go to that church anymore. You can't find your cross or quote a scripture if your life depended on it—been gone away from the church so long your pastor dare not ask you to lead the church in prayer—and the one tongue you have is so profane. You'll forget where you are and flip off a few at him in church. And you think you got it going on—man, get out of here with that mess. You better ask somebody.

I am convinced if a man doesn't have a conscience for God and the things of God, no other relationship will truly matter to him. Not mother, father, wife, or children will take precedence over his things. So, my sister, if you really want to see how much a man is committed to you, put him in a position to choose between you and his things, and see who will win.

I have searched desperately in the defendant's book to see a light on the hill—even a little salt would do. However, I have not been able to remotely find any semblance of God. Just mentioning His name is not enough. The proof is in the pudding.

Like I said before, I would be the first to agree that the Ten Commandments are extremely hard for anyone to keep. However, they are there to help us and not hurt us. They're a mirror into our souls and an assurance of our reliance on God. Don't be fooled; I am not issuing a license to sin—and we might sin. However, know this, God does not want us to become habitual sinners. He does not want us to be sinning like there's no tomorrow. If we continue on a sin-filled pattern, sin will have no effect on us, and the need for repentance will be foreign to us. We will be deemed serial sinners. Sin will be the killer of our souls. Man up. If one wants to do what most call cheating, just do it. It's who you are. Stop making excuses.

Note: Return to your first love and treat your spouse the way you did when you first met. Do the things you did to get them so you can keep them. That is the goal, right?

COUNT 6

MEN ARE SPORTS FISH
OR KEEPERS TOO

THE DEFENDANT HAS taken the liberty to relegate the clichéd title of "sports fish" or "keeper" to women. To the contrary, it is my belief that more men fall into this category than women. Of the many women that I have spoken to, the number-one complaint is trying to find a man worth putting in some hot grease and cooking. Unfortunately, when a woman catches a man, after careful observation, his brain ends up being one dimensional—his equipment is too small, his stamina is too short, he is unreliable, he has too many rough edges—and therefore, he is deemed good for only one thing: eye candy. So, when I reference a sports fish or keeper in this case, know that men are included in this conversation.

I believe one of the major problems we are faced with today is determining a keeper based off one's own standards—not who your mother, father, or homeboy or girlfriend thinks is good for you. Further, what's a keeper for you may not be a keeper for the next person. However, that doesn't mean the person is not a keeper. One man's junk can be another man's treasure. Many fishermen have thrown back fish that may have contained a pearl in its belly, thereby missing out on the blessing they have been waiting for, only to end up with a shark with teeth as sharp as nails.

The 4-1-1: Just because a woman dresses, talks, or walks in a certain way doesn't mean she's not a keeper—it's all a matter of preference.

DATING AND SOCIAL CLASS

TOO OFTEN, MANY people find themselves trying to date outside of their social class—and yes, it is such a thing. When rejected, they leave the situation feeling victimized. The rejected normally assumes that the rejecter feels they're too good for them. However, that's not always the case. Typically, when it's the male who feels rejected, the woman is attacked with an onslaught of insulting words meant to demean her character. Boys, we need to grow up someday—it may as well be today.

Folks, opposites only attract in the movies. It makes for a good storyline, but this is real life. It is extremely rare two people from different social classes will make a connection—unless it is simply for the purpose of a booty call. So, my brothers, you've been warned. Don't get your feelings caught up and act like a fool when you are cut off. You were just a plaything.

However, sometimes the rejecter is merely putting on a front, trying to be something they are not—perpetrating a fraud. Thereby, the rejected becomes the victim of someone's ego and walks away feeling like a throwback. That doesn't mean you're a sports fish or throwback, and you shouldn't accept that title as your destination.

News Bulletin
Everyone in Atlanta is a Business Owner or a Millionaire

When I moved to Atlanta years ago, I immediately noticed something strange about my new surroundings. Everyone was either an entrepreneur or a business owner. Their way of attempting to convince me they were a business owner was to give me a business card. I had so many business cards I didn't know what to do with them. Then I thought, man, I must have really been missing something. If it is that easy to own a business, then I better get on board. When asked what type of business they owned, they had some very interested sayings: *Well you know, I just started this thing and it's about to blow up, you with me?* Ahh no! Or, *my plate is full and I really can't take on anymore projects.* Or, *my son is going to be the next big thing in basketball and we will be rolling in the money.*

Word to the wise: My sisters, if your son has been on the basketball team since the tenth grade and he is now in the twelfth and been in the game twice for thirty seconds a clip, he's going to be something, but it's not going to be the next MJ. Shoot, the two times he was in the game the only basket he scored was in the other team's basket, and you were jumping up and down like you lost your mind, talking about "that's my baby." The whole time the other parents were looking at you like you were crazy, and you couldn't understand why. So, if this description fits your son, buy him some flip-flops and science books and just thank God he's on the team. The next MJ he won't be.

Keeping it real, most of the people who were saying they were an entrepreneur couldn't spell the word if their life depended on it. They had absolutely no understanding of the word, nor did they know what it took to be one. It was merely the "in" thing to say at the time. My people, my elevator goes all the way up to the top floor. I am not a fool. You cannot blow smoke up my rear end and think I am clueless to your game. I am not built like that. I can see game before you spew it out of your mouth. So, be who you are. Stop faking the funk. If you don't like who you are, no one else will.

Now, if the truth be told, we all have been somebody's sports fish or throwback—including the defendant. I myself have been on the wrong end of that shotgun. And when I was a boy, being thrown back wasn't a good feeling until I understood it wasn't a bad reflection on me. I just wasn't the person they wanted to be with. And that's not a bad thing.

Sadly, some of us take pride in being a sports fish. We wouldn't have it any other way. It is what we have become accustomed to, and we dare not venture into the unknown. Not surprisingly, some of us have been taught the art of being a sports fish by our mothers, fathers, and television alike. We take delight in it and wave our sports-fish flag for all to see.

In this count, the accused advised women not to give out their number to a man too soon, so he won't perceive them as a throwback. Allow me to run some interference here. A woman giving a man she may be interested in getting to know her phone number early on isn't a sign of a throwback. After all, the phone has always been an effective way of getting to know someone before you step out with them. A lot can be gleaned about a person's character just by talking to them on the phone and engaging them in certain topics of discussion. For instance, politics, religion, sexuality, and the family institution are subjects capable of getting one to reveal who they really are, thereby giving one enough information to determine if they want to spend the time and money to pursue another meeting. In other words, one can nip it in the bud before it gets started.

Also, a man not calling a woman the very next day is not indicative of his level of interest. Some women view a man calling too soon as a sign of a desperation. Thus, it may be concluded based on what some call a woman's intuition that the man is desperate or a stalker. Moreover, too often some people think when someone ask for their number with the possibility of getting to know them that a person is to drop everything they're doing and give them their full attention. Let me speak for myself here. I don't know about you, but I had goals and aspirations long before you came along. And believe me, I don't intend on losing my mind over a woman and having my goals sidetracked. After all, I didn't ask to marry you. I simply asked to get to know you. Big difference. Let me say it again: I'm a man and not a boy. I don't fall in love with a woman the same way a boy does. So don't take it personally, ladies, if a man doesn't burn your phone up.

In addition, a man not introducing a woman to his family from Jump Street is neither here nor there. Some men have standards by which they adhere to with regard to meeting their family. Some men take pride in honoring those who they deem to love the most. Therefore, real men will place a shield of protection around those he deems important to him, especially his parents and children.

For example, my mother and daughter are the most important people in my life. I take it very seriously when it comes to allowing a woman to meet them. I use a specific set of rules and reasoning to determine if a woman will meet my family or not. Allow me to share them with you:

Rule #1: If we're not engaged and don't have a wedding date set, you will never meet my family. Nor do I want to meet your family.

Reasoning #1: Seeing the importance of my mother and daughter to me, I don't want to disrespect them by bringing multiple women around them. I don't want my mother to feel like she has raised a whore for a son. In addition, I don't want my daughter to think it is okay for a man to be spreading himself thin all over the place. I understand that I'm my daughter's main role model and how I carry myself around her will impact her values concerning relationships.

Practice What I Preach: In the eighteen years since my divorce from my daughter's mother, I have never introduce any other woman to my daughter. Why? I don't know if you're going to be around, so what's the point? Moreover, my daughter is twenty-two years old, and she will never met anyone I'm involved with unless we have a ring and a date for marriage. To prove it, I'm willing to bet every dime I have that my daughter couldn't name any woman I've been involved with if you offered her a million dollars. I just don't operate like that.

I recall a time when a woman I was dating wondered why I wouldn't introduce her to my daughter. She asked me if I thought my daughter was too good for her to meet. I replied by saying, "Yes." She got offended, but I didn't give a good. . . . That was her issue to deal with.

We must began to understand the damaging psychological effects of introducing multiple mates to our children. It's confusing to them and, in some cases, can cause them to believe they're the reason we can't keep a mate. Unfortunately, sometimes these feelings can lead to depression and, in some cases, may result in the child committing suicide. More will be revealed on the subject of introducing your children to someone in a count titled "If He's Meeting Your Children before You Have a Ring and a Date, It's Too Soon."

My sisters, I understand a lot of you desire to have a man around the house. However, we must be extremely careful as to who we invite into our homes. Everything isn't always what it appears to be on the surface. We owe it to our children to provide a safe and productive home, so they can mature into the outstanding adults we know they can be. Be careful, don't let your desperation for lust be the cause for your making a decision that may cause your child their life. My heart aches every time I watch the news and see a boyfriend take his girlfriend's child's life. Ladies, you see how serious this issue can be?

Understand this: It's not that I'm not serious about a woman; I just believe there is a time and a season for everything. Besides, I might find out I don't like you as a person. So why put my family through the motions? And remember, one man's reasoning isn't another man's reasoning.

Note: A person's life doesn't stop just because they met someone they may be interested in. These assumptions are misleading and can cause someone who feeds off this garbage to miss their blessing. Don't be hoodwinked by fast talkers.

This carnal method (worldview) of determining if one is a keeper or not will never stand the test of time. Look at the divorce rate in this country. I'm pretty sure many of those who are divorced went through the same procedures the accused is describing. A divorce rate as high as it is today is only evident that this method employed to determine if one is a keeper or not is flawed. I believe the only way two people can identify a keeper is to study God's word, so they can identify the attributes God designed suitable for a keeper.

Warning: When I use the word *girl*, I am referring to a girl stuck in a grown woman's body. I'm not talking about your eight-year-old daughter. I'm talking about a woman with a girl's mind.

The ability of a woman to present herself as a lady or a girl is as far as the east is from the west. This lack of women being able to present themselves in a manner that would attracted men with more than sex on their minds is a result of a time period in which some women failed at their responsibility of being a role model to their daughters. As a result, too many women today are misguided as to what it takes to be a keeper.

Remember the 80s when young black girls led the teen-pregnancy rate in this country? During this period, too many senior grandmothers were left holding the bag. As the children grew older, the grandmothers couldn't do anything with them. This is the generation of women we see walking around here with their breast and booty hanging out for anybody to see. There was no one to teach them how to become a lady. And yes, it is the responsibility of mature ladies to teach the younger women how to become a lady, as seen in Titus 2:4–6:

> … *That they may teach the young women to be sober, to love their husbands, to love their children. To be discreet, chaste, keepers at home, good, obedient to their own husband, that the word of God be not blasphemed. . . .*

Keep in mind, one can't teach something they don't know. Nor can one take someone where one has never been. If a woman has never been taught how to be a lady, she has nothing to pass on to her young daughter. The cycle will continue to perpetuate itself, and things will get worst as time goes on.

Keep in mind, it's important for a woman to carry herself in the manner of a lady at all times. One will never know when God will present you to your husband. So don't degrade yourself five minutes before your blessing comes. Have patience and wait on the Lord. He will always provide for you.

By the way, for someone who occasionally refers to God in his writings, I have yet to see any evidence in his book based on the principals of God when it comes to relationships. Why is that? Like I said, you can't teach something you don't know. You can't be blind to God's word and give out directions to paradise. It takes skill and patience to read the blueprint of God. So be extremely careful as to whose table you sit down at and brake bread. They may be cooking your meal with dirty hands. And everything that tastes good isn't good for you.

A Lady versus a Girl

A Few Examples of the Differences

- Girls will drop something on the ground in public and bend over with their tails in the air for anyone to see. A lady, on the other hand, will scoot down with her bottom to the ground and pick up what she dropped in one motion and keep it moving. Lusters will be standing their upset because she didn't display her goodies to them.

- Girls will sit in front of strange men with their legs wide open as if she wants them to see. A lady will sit up straight with her legs closed, and you would have to kill her just to get a peek.

- A girl will grab, beat, embarrass, and threaten her children in public for something a child will do by nature. A lady will look down at her child and say, "You know you're going to get it when Daddy gets home." The child will look up at mommy and say, "I'm sorry, Momma. Can you please punish me instead of Daddy?"

- A girl will wear the most outrageous hairstyle she can possibly come up with. A lady will wear something conservative and let her true beauty speak for her.

- A girl will come out of the house with spandex pants on, and everyone can clearly see her goodies—thong and all. A lady will come outside with her spandex pants on, and she will have something over top of them. You might not even know she has them on. If you can see them, you will be left with only your imagination.

- A girl will come outside with rollers in her hair for everyone to see. By the way, that's not appealing at all. A lady won't even come to the mailbox with rollers in her hair. She'll send her husband to get the mail instead.

- A girl will open the door and walk in before a man when he's standing right there. A lady won't touch the door and will give you a look that demands you open the door for her. She will never reach for that handle. I know this to be true. Two ladies did this exact thing to me at the mall. The only thing I could do was open the door and laugh . . . and they said thank you.
- A girl won't leave anything to a man's imagination. With a lady, all you're going to have is your imagination.
- A girl will gloat if a man addresses her as sweetie, sexy, honey, or baby. A lady, without hesitation, will put that man is his place. And she will have her finger on the 9-1-1 speed dial just in case you have a problem.
- A girl will promote her body as her centerpiece; that's all she has. A lady's centerpiece is her mind, body, and soul; she has the total package.
- A girl will even destroy the wearing of a sweat suit—she just has to show her breasts. A lady will even make a sweat suit look classy.
- Some girls will spray the whole bottle of perfume on them before they leave the house. They'll even squirt some down low—I thought a bath took care of that area. They do this so any man can pick up their scent. A lady, on the other hand, will put very small amounts of perfume on her. Why? She's only trying to have the one for her pick up her scent. She's not going to let just anyone get close to her. And even if you're the one she wants to smell her scent, you better not get too close, because she will push you away and put you in your place.

From My Childhood: Growing up, I did everything all the other boys liked to do. We played sports, rode bikes, raised pigeons, and raised dogs. However, raising dogs was the boy-man thing to do. Although raising dogs was the thing to do, most boys didn't like raising female dogs—myself included. Reason being, when a female dog was in heat, her scent could be smelled throughout the neighborhood, and it would attract large groups of dogs—sound familiar?

Occasionally a stray dog in heat would get loose, and her scent would set off a frenzy, resulting in a pack of wild dogs trying to see who could get the first piece. Some dogs would even fight one another to see who could get to the finish line first. More often than not, her efforts to avoid being slaughtered were to no avail. The dogs would circle her, push and bite one another, until finally, the dominant male would get there first. The dog that has the "who I am, what I have, and where I'm going" mentality.

Through all of this, I realized the female dog really only wanted one dog to follow her scent. She had her eyes on one, and the others were just in the way. However, in the process of warding off the unwanted dogs, she would on occasion turn around and wait until the one she wanted would get in position and then she gave in—she was waiting to exhale. The moral to this story is this: even though she was a dog—she was a lady-dog.

WHAT GIRLS LOOK FOR VERSUS WHAT LADIES LOOK FOR

WHAT GIRLS LOOK FOR!
- Is he cute?
- What kind of car does he drive?
- Can he get me some free food from his job?
- Can he pay my forty-dollar phone bill?
- Is he a sucker?
- Can I slush off of him? In other words, can I live off him for free?
- Do he wear the latest fashions?
- Is he good in bed?
- Will my girlfriends like him?

WHAT LADIES LOOK FOR!

- Do he have a career? Not a job.
- Is he educated?
- Can he take care of a family?
- Do he have benefits (health insurance, etc.)?
- What is his credit score?
- Will he take care of me if I get sick?
- Does he make regular doctor visits?
- What investments does he have?
- Does he any goals?
- Does he live in a house, apartment, or with his momma?
- Is he renting or buying?
- Does he keep himself groomed?
- How many children does he have? And are they by different women?
- Does he pay his bills on time?
- What kind of relationship does he have with his mother?
- What is his debt-to-equity ratio?
- Can he hold a stimulating conversation?
- Is he politically aware?
- Does he have confidence in himself?
- Is he resourceful?

THE COMPARISONS I have just made are not one-hundred-percent proof positive. They're meant to make one think. However, by using some of the examples above, one can pause for a second, take a look in the mirror, and ponder if their appearance is that of a lady or a girl. But don't be deceived. A female may have the appearance of a lady; however, Satan comes in many forms. He is the deceiver of all deceivers. Satan invented the art of deception; he is good at what he does—deception is his motto—and he very much enjoys doing what he does.

The thief cometh not, but for to steal, and to kill, and to destroy: I come that they may have life, and that they might have it more abundantly.

(JOHN 10:10)

Satan will lie to you, steal from you, kill you, and then destroy any evidence of your existence. No one will ever know you lived. If you don't believe me, talk to a Fire Chief about the motives of a criminal who burns down a house. The criminal breaks in, steals the spoils, kills the occupants, and then burns down the house to erase the existence of everything within, including the people who lived there.

Therefore, it would behoove one not to base their decision on appearance alone. It would be wise to match the actions of a man or woman with the words that are coming out of his or her mouth. And please don't take the advice of the very type of men women are complaining about. Pray, use the wisdom of God, and don't be duped by those who talk loud but have nothing coming out of their mouths. Do it God's way, and it will last to the end of the earth.

MY TEST FOR A KEEPER

SOME MANY MOONS ago, God gave to me an ironclad sign to determine if a woman was sent to me from Him or not. He said that if I go by this measuring stick, I will never go wrong. He stated this to me as sure as He lives. Here's what He said to me:

If a woman opens her legs up to you before marriage, know that I didn't send her. I said, why, Lord? Everybody else is testing the waters. He said, first, I called you to be my defender. I cannot have you filled with great sin. The lust of sex is a demon that will pull you to your knees. It will weaken your preaching and my words that come from you will fall on deaf ears.

Second, if a woman doesn't honor her body with you, she will dishonor her body with anyone. That's not the one I have for you. You need someone who totally honors her body and will be committed to you until death do you part. If a woman joins allegiance with you on this matter, she will stick by you and stand with you in the face of adversity just as my son and daughter Adam and Eve did: They stuck together even when they had to face me. That is exactly what I designed a man and a woman to do.

Check this out!

For centuries, theologians, scholars, preachers, and laymen have overlooked the fact that Adam and Eve stuck together in the face of God. It has always been the tradition to point out the blame game in this dispensation. No one has ever given notice to the fact that Adam and Eve were joined at the hip. This blame-game dilemma is common among us all when trying to assess responsibility for wrongdoing—just ask a marriage counselor.

Words of wisdom: Know this, if you're married and you had sex with your spouse before you got married, God wasn't there. I would suggest that you and your spouse seriously repent and ask God to clean up your marriage. He is the only one who can do it. It wouldn't be a bad idea to fast for as long as He directs you, to show your commitment. Why?

You invited the devil to join you at the altar. So don't wonder how he's able wreak havoc in your family. All he needs is a crack, and he will slide right on in. Have faith. God can restore your marriage to a state of acceptance. Don't be fooled by the wiles of Satan and his cohorts. Any sex outside of the ordinances of God is casual sex. It's that plain and simple.

Now, my ladies, I need for you all to do me a favor. First, find a young woman and take her under your arm and teach her how to become a lady.

Men, do likewise. Find a young man and truly take him to the school of manhood. I believe we can conquer this dilemma one young person at a time. If you participate in this venture, I'm sure you'll feel pretty good you helped someone. Men are sports fish or keepers too.

COUNT 7

STRONG AND INDEPENDENT
WOMEN: WHY NOT?

I N A P R E V I O U S count to his case, I recall the woman's voice advising women to listen to him over the advice of their mothers. He claims to understand men better, over the many years of experience of our mothers. Now he's suggesting in this count that the reason women are so independent is because of the advice given to them by the smart women in their lives. It's about time he got something right.

However, according to the defendant, this is even wrong. Why? He states, "Unless a woman allows a man to fulfill his role as a man by providing for her, he will not feel like a man and will eventually leave—hit the road, Jack." Normally, this response to a successful woman stems from several things much deeper than feeling like a man. Let me explain it to you.

A man's ego, his jealousy, his lack of ability to control, and his insecurities within himself, more often than not, play a key role in his inability to accept the reality of the day, and emerge from the Dark Ages. In other words, some women just plain-old got it going on. And a lot of men can't handle that. Face the music, brothers. Some of us are still sleepwalking. Power to the sister!

Along with the aforementioned shortcomings of some men, I will show you that the mothers of strong, independent, and successful women had good reason to teach their daughters to be able to provide for themselves. History has taught many women the detriment of not being able to provide for their own well-being. In times past, as a result of not being able to provide for themselves, many women have found themselves in some of the most abusive situations imaginable. Some women were beaten to death, or near death; some women were verbally murdered; some women were sexually murdered; some women were treated as if their worth was less than that of an animal; and the men who were committing these crimes were the very men these women thought loved them. Therefore, it behooved mothers to ensure their daughters would not have to suffer the same inhumane treatment they experienced. Mama, I'm not mad with you—with your fourth-grade education and PhD in God's wisdom.

Be advised, my brothers, I am not sitting here trying to see if I can make up a story to impress women. The previous statements are true beyond a shadow of a doubt. As a matter of fact, I myself have firsthand knowledge of an abusive father. My dad abused my mother. I saw him beat my mother, degrade her both publically and privately—in front of family and friends—and rob her finances to support a whorish lifestyle with the many different women which he made no attempt to hide. But check this out!

A Son's Love: Many people work out for different reasons. Some people work out for health reasons; some people work out because they want to look good; some people work out for sports; and some people work out for the sheer enjoyment. A lot of my friends think I work out for some of these same reasons—they're half right. However, my reason for working out is much more than those stated. Take a look.

During the period in which I experienced my dad abusing my mother, I realized I was too small to defend her. When I would attempt to get in the way, my mother showed no concern for her life in an effort to protect me from my dad. She placed herself in a position that made her defenseless to the assault of my father. Therefore, having enough of seeing my mother suffer, I began to work out in order to gain the size needed to defend my mother from my father. As I am sitting here writing this commentary, I can remember very vividly as if the event were taking place now.

I recall one day my mother racing into the house with my father in hot pursuit of her. My brother and I heard the commotion and we ran out of the room and stood at the top of the steps to see what was going on. As my dad started to come after my mother, she turned around and hurled a bottle at him. Enraged, my dad charged after her, and that's when my brother and I stepped in and put an end to the abuse of my mother. We had the size to protect her now, and promised him if he ever laid hands on our mother again, we would send him to his grave—we meant every word of it.

Further, the reason for a mother teaching a daughter to be independent doesn't stop there. Look at the alarming number of men and boys making babies and abandoning women to leave them with no option but to become independent. In this day and time, fathers have come up MIA at an alarming rate. Some fathers spread themselves so thin a song was named after them: "Papa Was a Rollin' Stone." Make a baby over here, make a baby over there, and make a baby everywhere. I believe this song to be one of the most degrading songs to women I've ever heard.

With so much empirical knowledge into the behavior of men, a woman would be foolish to entrust her total well-being to a man. If a woman allows it, history will repeat itself, and the same devastating experiences their mothers faced will show up at their door and steal every inch of dignity within their body.

Be advised, if you are in this position, or if you know someone in this position, here's my advice to you: You have too many resources at your disposal to allow any man to treat you like a dog. 9-1-1 is there for you; women's battered shelters are there for you; your family is there for you; and if need be, you can escape to a friend's house. Hell, if I had a friend who was in this situation, she could escape to my house—and I wish her husband would come to my house with some of his bull-shiggady.

My sisters, whatever you do, don't just sit there and make excuses for why you can't leave. Take the first step to recovery and get as far away from that place as possible. I will assure you, the moment you leave, a huge burden will be lifted off your back, and you will taste the blessing of being free. Look to the hills whence cometh your help. He will never leave you nor forsake you.

Now, let's look at some of the other problems men have with successful women. To their disadvantage, some men still believe women are subservient to them and that women need men to fix things. Therefore, a woman should sit, look pretty, and do whatever a man tells her to do, whenever a man tells her to do it, and how a man tells her to do it. Does this sound familiar? It should.

What's really going on? It's the control factor. As stated above, a major characteristic of an abuser is his ability to control the abused. He controls the money, where the abused goes and when they go, and who the abused is around and when they're around them. Fortunately, a woman who is financially stable is able to get up and leave without any fear of how she's going to make it. This factor is not good for the barbaric thinkers of old. They have lost their power to control and now feel less than a man. My sisters, keep doing what you're doing. Nobody's mad but the devil.

Next, let's deal with the issue of a man's ego. A man's ego is first cousin to pride. Too often a man's pride evolves into conceit. It even becomes haughty, and his woman isn't excluded from this experience. What I have, who I am, and where I'm going. These traits at some point will reveal themselves in a nasty way. *I did this for you, and you mean to tell me you're not going to give me any of the goodies? I paid your bills . . . I bought you a new car . . . you live in a house your girls only wish they lived in . . . and you wear the finest clothes of all women.* And the best is yet to come. *Because of who I am, what I have, and where I'm going, you should be grateful just to be in my presence.*

As you can see, a strong and independent woman doesn't have to put up with this mess. She has her own and can get up and leave when she gets good and ready. She can toot her own horn, strut her stuff, and flip a man the bird on her way out the door. This is a problem for most men's ego.

Once again, they lose control and must deal with the defeat of standing up to the archaic definition of what entails manhood. It is what it is, my brothers. The women of the world call it "Women Power." Don't hate; appreciate.

Then we have the issue of jealousy. Some men think being the head means being the best at everything. A woman is not supposed to be able to do the things some believe were meant for a man to do. That's sad. As I stated at the beginning of this case, a woman is nothing but a man with a womb. Which means, she has the ability to do everything a man can do—profess her love, provide for her family, protect her family.

Here's my belief: The problem comes when a man sees a woman doing something better than him that we think men are supposed to do better than women. News flash, fellas: I have seen some women who are much better at fixing things around the house than I am. And I don't feel less than a man. She just knows how to do what she know how to do. And I ain't mad at her. Why? That means it's less I have to do. Go on, girl. Do your thing. I's gonna sit here and be your cheering section. My pride ain't hurt at all.

Let me indulge you for a second on a topic that's popular within Christian circles. Are you familiar with the belief that in order for two people to be considered compatible for marriage they must be equally yoked? Let me give you some Wharton Theology on this subject. Here's what this means:

To be equally yoked means to link up with someone who is a believer—that's it. However, when coming together as one, it's good when one possess something their partner is lacking. In other words, if your spouse knows how to do the budget, and you don't, she's in charge of the budget. If you know how to invest, and she doesn't, you're in charge of the investing. If your wife knows how to cook better than you, you get in there with her and learn so you can give her a break sometimes, and clean the kitchen when you're finish. If your wife makes more money than you, so be it. She did what she had to do to get where she is. Accept it, be proud of her, get over your boyish pride, and give credit where credit is due.

Additionally, another pie that's baked in the oven of a man with regard to strong and independent women is insecurity. He knows he can't control her or undermine her—he knows she can do it just as good as he can do it—and he knows there are plenty of men standing in line waiting for a chance with that heavenly sent woman. Sadly, his manhood tells him, because his woman doesn't need him, he's not a man. Get over that *bull----* already.

For the record, my manhood is not tied into who I am, what I have, and where I'm going. My manhood is directly related to my character, to what makes me who I am. For instance, how do I carry myself outside the presence of those who are important to me?

- Do I cheat on my wife?
- Do I flirt with her girlfriends when she's not around?
- Do I help her with the nurturing of our children and not view it as drudgery or a chore?
- Do I rub her feet for her and not expect goodies in return?
- Do I open the car door for her even though I am upset with her?
- Will I go out of my way to keep my family together at all cost?
- And last, but not least, do I take charge in the spiritual nurturing of my family?

These are just a few things that are the heart and soul of a true man. A true man will put aside all appearances of control, jealousy, ego, and insecurities to fulfill the true purpose of a man. That's keeping the family together at all cost, no matter what anyone outside of the family thinks.

THINGS A STRONG INDEPENDENT
WOMAN LOOKS FOR IN A MAN

- Does a man have the ability to step in and take over if some misfortune should occur to her? In other words, will he be able to sustain the lifestyle she has become accustomed to?
- Having the ability, will he step in and take over?
- Is he the type of man who will view a woman's misfortune as an opportunity to assert control over her?
- Is he the type of man that will throw everything he does for a woman in her face?
- Will he be supportive in her efforts to regain her status?
- Will he maintain the same level of respect for her if she becomes more successful than him?
- Will he complain about having to do it all?
- Will he be fainthearted and seek someone else to replace what she is no longer able to provide.

These are very real questions a strong and independent woman will confront when deciding if she'll date a man. I know some men may have a problem with this train of thought, but it's logical, reasonable, and just good common sense for a woman to ask these questions. And for the low self-esteem, when a successful woman doesn't want to be with your *broke* ---, it's not because a woman thinks she's too good for you. It's because of what she likes, what she knows, and what makes her happy. And by all accounts, a woman has every right to seek that which she deems will make her happy. So get over your insecurities. You knew from the first moment you laid eyes on that woman those stars were too high for you to reach. Learn how to separate fact from fiction, and you won't ever have to worry about assuming a woman thinks she's too good for you. Some things only happen in the movie.

MY SONG

I AIN'T GOT A PROBLEM WITH A
WOMAN HELPING OUT

I ain't got a problem with a woman helping out—I ain't got a problem with her helping with the bills. I ain't got a problem with a woman buying dinner—'cause that's what lets me know I got me a winner. I ain't got a problem with a woman driving me in the car—that just makes me feel like star. I ain't got a problem with a woman treating me like a king—that lets me know I'm gonna have to treat her like a queen. Do you know what I mean? I ain't got a problem with a woman asking me to rub her feet—because I know when she's ready it's going to benefit me. I ain't got a problem with my woman making the plans—because I know she's always going to do the best she can. I ain't got a problem with my woman handling the money—just as long as the money don't come up funny. I ain't got a problem with my woman leading the pack—because I'm sure capable of picking up the slack. I ain't got a problem with a woman deciding things—just in case you didn't know that's one of the roles of a queen. I AIN'T GOT A PROBLEM WITH A STRONG AND INDEPENDENT WOMAN. My manhood is intact. Peace out.

COUNT 8

GOD'S RULE

And be not conformed to this world: but be ye transformed
by the renewing of your mind, that ye may prove what is
that good, and acceptable, and perfect, will of God
ROMANS 12:2

W OW! NINETY DAYS. I'm really going to have a lot of respect
for you. If ninety days is all the respect a woman has for herself,
that's not saying much; and no true man is going to hold her in high regards
either. This is one of the most asinine theories I have ever heard. However,
I'm not surprised. Look who it came from.

So what is this rule? Here it goes: "Ladies, don't give a man sex before
ninety days. If you do, he won't have respect for you and won't stick around
for the long-haul." This theory is known as the woman's voice probationary
period for determining if a man is worthy of her goodies. In other words,
if a woman holds out for ninety days before giving a man her goodies,
she will be able to determine if a man is worthy of the benefits of being
employed by her. Well, I stopped by to tell you that's a lie straight from
the pits of hell.

Under this system of logic, the only thing we have achieved is an
astronomical divorce rate. It is extremely rare people will be successful
in a relationship by this standard. Most marriages that are orchestrated

outside the guidelines of God fail before they begin to take flight. By the way, just because a marriage lasted for forty years doesn't mean God had anything to do with it.

Let's use the analogy employed by the defendant to illustrate how an employer determines if a prospective employee is worthy of the employer's benefits. Check this out!

The employer uses a ninety-day probationary period to determine if an employee is worthy of his benefits. During this period, the employer observes the employee's job performance. The employer monitors the employee's on-time performance, the employee's absenteeism rate, the employee's ability to complete assignments on time, the employee's willingness to work with others, etc. It's been ninety days. Mr. So-and-So, you now get the benefits.

To the contrary, history states that the only thing sticking around for ninety days proves is one has stamina for ninety days— that's it. Further, I don't know about anyone else, but I've been working since I was eighteen, and I can testify to this: I don't have enough fingers and toes on my body to count the number of times I've seen employees come and go after ninety days. Why is this?

We all have worked on jobs we thought were the best thing since sliced bread. The job had plenty of vacation time, medical benefits, an excellent dental plan, a pension fund, stock options—the whole nine yards. No valley was low enough and no mountain was too high to climb. We were in employment heaven. We could walk on water and felt like we were on cloud nine and God had finally answered our prayers. As a matter of fact, we were so happy our disposition was as such: "How do you like me now?!" we bragged to our friends, then called home, told Mama, and walked around with our chest stuck out and our heads held high in the air like a proud peacock. "I have arrived!"

Then we get that call from our homeboy or girlfriend telling us about another position across town we need to check out. And how many of you all know, when we check out something, we check out. We check out the position and realize this position is the one we've always wanted. During the interview process we talk the talk and get offered the position. We said all the right things—just like we did with our present job.

However, to our present employer's surprise (our woman), as soon as we leave the interview, we begin to think about all the wonderful things we said at the interview to our present employer. The promises of commitment we swore by and the unmatched energy we exhibited at work every day. We put in extra hours, never showed up for work late, and took on extra assignments. Suddenly, we begin to reason within ourselves to justify disappointing our present employer who put so much confidence in our bull. . . . And we all know, because we're not man enough to face them, we give them our resignation over the phone. And finally, we tell ourselves it was only a job, not a career. It only served a purpose for the moment, so what the hell if they get upset? Sound familiar to anyone?

So, as you can see, qualifying for your benefits does not mean a man is committed to keeping them. They may look at you as a temporary employment assignment, not a career—big difference.

Well, folks, it works the same way in a lot of relationships. The man starts off by saying and doing all the right things. He helps you with your kids, shows up for work on time, does all the other extra assignments you ask of him, fixes your car, paints your house, goes for walks in the park, takes you to concerts and art exhibits, and he even takes you to the restaurant where he can't pronounce the names of the entrees on the menu. And, to top it off, he even picks up your kids from school and takes them to soccer practice. You're so happy you start bragging to your girls about how you think you finally found the one—God has answered your prayers. Your co-workers even notice the change in your attitude at work. You're singing, whistling, strutting into the office bouncing, and you even offer to buy lunch—something you never do. Your co-workers think you done lost your mind.

Unexpectedly, you get the dreaded call. He informs you he really liked working for you, but he found the career he's always been looking for and can't pass up the opportunity. He begins to tell you about the benefits of the other employer: better breasts, bigger booty, less stress, and no baby-daddy drama. You get upset and begin to express your disappointment. To your dismay, somebody other than the man you thought you knew stands up. He tells you how sorry he is to disappoint you, but he says to your bewilderment, "See you and I wouldn't want to be you." Your jaw hits the floor, and you're left in total shock wondering, how could he do this to me? Ninety days—that's how—way too soon. Am I on somebody's street?

Let's look at this from another angle. If a man's desire for sex is as strong as the expert claims, I hope my sisters aren't foolish enough to believe that, while you're implementing this ninety-day program, a man is waiting for you—actually some men do. Unfortunately for some, nine times out of ten, men will not wait. He's probably got someone on the side who is willing to give him a thrill until you decide to give in. It is not in the character of boy-men like the self-proclaimed woman's voice to give that type of allegiance to a woman—it ain't going to happen. That thought is far from anything their mind can conjure up. Stop being hoodwinked!

Note: There's an Old Latin proverb which states, "Things that are written remain."

With that in mind, God's probationary period for intimacy was etched in stone many moons ago. The decision for when couples are to know one another is neither the man's nor the woman's—it's God's. He has decided the blueprint for knocking boots, and we earn the right to be with one another when we do it according to the bylaws of God.

According to the defendant's Ninety-Day Rule the woman is the one who decides when physical intimacy is to take place. As a result of this school of thought, some women believe their bodies are on a higher plaque than a man's, a notion that too many men have aided. Hence, the system of a woman's benefit and payment from being in a man's presence: I beg to differ. Besides, I've said it before, and I'm going to say it again,

"An even exchange is no robbery." Therefore, we both benefit from being in one another's presence.

Check point: A relationship isn't a one-way street. However, somewhere society has gone wrong. I know it is done out of flattery, but we have given women a false since of power they really don't have. We tell them they hold all power in their hands. The defendant in this case tried to demonstrate this theory by alluding to Eve being responsible for man's condition. In other words, Eve was given some imaginary power she didn't have. Wrong again.

First, the command not to eat from the tree was given to Adam and not Eve. Eve wasn't even around when the command was given. Second, because Adam had extensive knowledge of the things of the garden, he could identify everything in the garden blindfolded. So, when the fruit was presented to him, he should have known better than to eat from it. It was his responsibility to guard and protect the things of God, including his duty to protect his wife. He failed.

I tried to find something that would indicate Eve rammed the food down his throat. I had no luck. I think this is another case of man falling asleep on the job. Adam was told of the consequences of cheating on God—just like a man knows the consequences of cheating on a woman.

As I stated in a previous section, Adam, like men who cheat, made his own choices. It doesn't just happen, and it is within one's power to choose the opposite. Although, nothing to the contrary being identified, it appears to me they had a mutual agreement to eat from that tree. The same way a man and a woman must mutually agree to be in a relationship. That choice is not solely in the power of the woman.

Let's take a look at this from the prospective of the game of chess. The king is the target of the chess game. "Kill the head and the body will follow," so they say. The most important and most powerful ally to the king is the queen. She has the ability to protect the king like no other piece on the board. Therefore, it would behoove the king to include the queen in on everything going on in the house, including the standards for getting married. This tells me, if Eve brought Adam some food from the tree he wasn't supposed to eat from, evidently he didn't give her full details as to the detriment of that tree. Once again, failing at his duty to keep and protect.

God's Probationary Period

A FAMOUS FOOTBALL PLAYER spoke out about God's probationary period and he got it right. However, when a man takes a stance against the issue of pre-marital sex, the normal response of society is to label that individual and attempt to make a mockery of him. They began to tag him and question his sexuality—especially some women.

See if any of these sayings sound familiar: *He's weird; something must be wrong with him; can't no man go without a woman; he's crazy for even trying that foolishness*; and—the all-time favorite of some women—*he must be gay*.

Not surprising, however, this sentiment is even shared among most American Christians. Why? Sex before marriage among Christians is so common and acceptable in the church, little attention if any is given to this topic from most pulpits. I can't recall in my thirty-year stint with the church ever hearing a message denouncing fornication. Moreover, a man can get some booty out of the church faster than he can from a night club. Even worse, I never imagined in my wildest dream a man would be able to sleep with a woman and never know her last name—church women are not excluded. Holy cow!

This Ninety-Day Rule reminds me of another idiotic rule some women have before they decide to sleep with a man. This rule is called the "Five Date Rule." Similar to the Ninety-Day Rule, this rule states a felonious time frame as to when a woman should give into a man. It's simple: A woman shouldn't give a man sex until she's been out on at least five dates with him. If she follows this procedure, a man will respect her and she will be able to tell if he is serious about her. Somebody please tell me that's a joke. It's not.

Breaker-Breaker 1-9: My sisters, if that isn't being shortchanged, I don't know what is.

As you will see later on in this book (Count 11: "The Mark of the High Calling"), I used a pictorial to illustrate the correct way and the wrong way as to how a woman can reach her mark. In the wrong way illustration, the format used by some women coincides with this present philosophy of how a woman is to keep a man: meet someone, go on five dates, and then the booty—that's cheap. My homeboy June Bug can foot that bill.

Player-Player from the Himalayas: Allow me to inform the world of women who adhere to this school of thought of a very important piece of information. If a man were a player balling in money, to pay for five dates would be the sum of paying for a prostitute. He would look at the money spent on five dates as an expense of sleeping with a woman to do his business—just like a prostitute—nothing more, and nothing less. He would allow a woman to think she is really doing something, when in turn, all he's doing is waiting for her to drop her panties. And trust me, they're eventually going to come off. It's just a matter of time.

So, who's the blame for this dilemma? It is men's fault that some of our women feel they must succumb to such low standards in order to get a man. Black men have failed their responsibility to uplift the African Queen to her rightful status in the home and society. Sadly, we have become the new face of the slave master to our women. We bring our women in by ship loads and place them on the auction block in very much the same way the slave masters did during slavery days. How?

We summon them into the night club half-neck'ed, go over them from head to toe with a fine-tooth comb, and assess them to see which one would be fit to be our slave. We look to see who has the biggest booty, breast, and fairest skin as factors to help us make our decision. After we win the bid, much like the slave master, we take them home and do as we please with them. We fulfill our lustful desire, we impregnate them, and then we have the audacity to throw them to the dogs and leave them for some other man to take care of the baby. My brothers, we are the new face of the slave master—

"Objection, your honor!" the defense interjects.

"Order in the court!" the judge replies. "Mr. Wharton, you keep telling it like it is."

This scenario was brought to fruition for me when I was at a club with an associate of mine. Unbeknownst to us, we went on a night when the women at the club were more than half our age. I immediately notice the difference in age and instantly felt out of place. I knew my being there would render me absolutely nothing. My associate, however, was very satisfied with what he saw—and we all know what that was. I, on the other hand, could only see my twenty-two-year-old daughter in the young women he was lusting over. I tried to no avail to get my associate to see what I was seeing—he was not having it. Just so everyone is clear, I made sure my associate knew how disgusted I was and informed him—I don't roll like that. And, no, I'm not cutting him loose. Why? I just might be the agent to get him to see differently. I'm working on him. And trust me, it's hard to get a boy-man to look past breast and booty.

My brothers, it's a shame I must explain this to grown men in 2014. Our women are more than just a piece of meat, and we must start at once demonstrating it to them. We also must remember that everything we do to women is a reflection of how we feel about ourselves. She is bone of our bones and flesh of our flesh. When we look at our women we are only looking at ourselves—with a slight difference. And, when we disrespect and cheat on our women, we're only doing it to ourselves. Let the church say amen.

My sisters, you need to help in the case as well. Put some clothes on— cover up, wear a longer dress, sit with your legs closed before men—and demand the respect you deserve.

Our satisfaction with failed relationships must be eradicated. We have obtained such a level of comfort with failing in our relationships it's really no big thing anymore. It is the expected outcome, and no one is bothered by it.

Before I moved to Georgia eighteen years ago, I was accustomed to failing. I failed in all my relationships, jobs, school, and as a Christian. As a matter of fact, it was expected of me to fail by all who knew me. So when I failed, it was no big thing. My logic was, I was a creature of habit, and I was only doing the thing I was accustomed to doing—failing.

It wasn't until I moved to Georgia that an epiphany took place in my life and I saw I could do something else other than fail. That epiphany for me was seeing the many African American success stories up close and in person. I was meeting doctors, lawyers, politicians, successful business owners, etc. They had nice houses, cars, and a beautiful lifestyle. It was then I realized someone had been lying to me all the time. I admired the people I was meeting and believed if they could do it, so could I. It was then I began to change my way of thinking and start on my quest to learn something new. Thank you, Georgia!

My brothers and sisters, an epiphany must take place in our relationships if we're to turn this thing around any time soon. We must not continue in our comfort zone of failure if we're going to give our children the love of a family they deserve. The African King must be awakened from the tomb of the dead and heed the call to be the leader he was designed to be. Our women and children are counting on us to come and rescue them. I believe we can overcome this tragic situation one man and one woman at a time, if we just put our best foot forward. So, my brothers, take off the garments of the dead, come out of the tomb, and put on the soldier's uniform and prepare for battle. The stench from our tombs has ascended to the heavens, and God is not pleased.

The aforementioned theories of the Ninety-Day Rule and the Five-Date Rule must be eliminated from the dating playbook. If we continue to adhere to such fictitious principles, by the time we meet someone who is truly interested in something serious with us, we would've gone through so many people we won't be any good to anyone. It is beyond me to conjure in my mind the number of mates one can have over a fifty-year period by applying these standards. If we really want to have a successful relationship, we must reconsider the methods we're using to achieve that goal. Think on those things.

Before I go any further, let me make sure God's laws on fornication didn't change. Give me a second and let me check something out. Well, I'm sorry. It's still on the books.

> *Flee fornication. Every sin that a man doeth is without the body,*
> *but he that committeth fornication sinneth against his own body.*
>
> (1 CORINTHIANS 6:18)

I thought so. But I just wanted to be sure. So, as one can see, when we sin, we sin not only against God, but ourselves as well. And that's not good for anyone.

Look at this rule from another perspective. As stated earlier, God's laws state no sex before marriage. Has anyone tried that? Oh! We must test the waters first. Now remember, I'm talking to Christians, not heathens. I know you might be saying, "Why not heathens?" Well, to answer your question, Jesus excluded heathens from certain conversations. Rememeber the old aphorism: "Everything isn't for everybody." Besides, heathens love a lie better than the truth.

> *Let not your heart be troubled: ye believe in God, believe also in*
> *me. . . .*
>
> (JOHN 14:1–6)

In this passage of scripture, Jesus is talking to his disciples (Christians). No one else is around. Pagan worshipers aren't allowed to enter the camp of the saints. They will try to pollute the minds of the saints with their wicked ways. My present company is not excluded.

Deep down inside, when I think about this rule and those who comply with it, I think about the true message it sends. First, it tells me that some women are willing to allow the very men their complaining about to determine their worth. Second, it shows me how little the defendant thinks about women. Ninety days—that's all you're worth. And it shows me how little the women who follow this school of thought think of themselves. My sisters, you mean to tell me your cookie is only worth ninety days. Those are pretty low standards. That's easy. That's no real accomplishment, especially when a woman is on the side while a man is waiting for your Ninety-Day Rule to expire. Come on now.

God's Headlines:
What a Woman's Body is Really Worth.

And God saw everything that he had made, and behold, it was very good....

(GENESIS 1:31)

Let's see what this scripture is saying about women. Women are extraordinarily good—exceptionally good, magnificently good, good-good. In other words, a woman is like a piece of Kentucky Fried Chicken—finger-licking good. She's like a bag of M&M's chocolate—she melts in your mouth and not in your hand. Can I get a witness?

Let's look at this from another perspective. If the accused were a heart surgeon, with his success rate, would you allow him to perform surgery on you? He openly brags about his many failed relationships. That's nothing to brag about. Moreover, if he were a baseball player, with his batting average, he wouldn't make the cut. He would be considered a scrub. The coach of the team wouldn't even consider him for his D-league team. For my ladies who don't know sports, that's pretty bad.

This aptitude of reasoning shouldn't even be considered when a woman needs advice. I would suggest you go to the Bible or your mother if you really want to know the standards of lady-hood. There you can find all the experience you need in dealing with a man. Alternatively, find yourself a true man and talk to him. One who has proven his manhood and doesn't mind sharing it with you.

News Bulletin: I Just Met You

It is believed by the accused that a woman can tell if a man is serious about her if he does certain things within this ninety day probationary period. However, let's keep it real here.

It has been my experience that too many people when you first meet them have a belief that your world should stop on account of them. You're to forget everything you had going on and devote all your time, energy, and money to them. And if you don't, you're not serious about them.

I'm sorry, ladies, it just doesn't work that way for a lot of men. It doesn't work that way for me. You've been hoodwinked. I asked you out to get to know you. Getting to know someone doesn't require a man to spend ridiculous amounts of time and money on a woman to prove his interest in her. I didn't ask you for your hand in marriage. Besides, like I stated earlier, I might not even like you. It takes more than ninety days for me to ascertain whether or not I want to be in a committed relationship with a woman. So, a man asking you out isn't a proclamation of love.

Moreover, before you came around (and this might surprise some), I had goals, bills, and a life outside of you. No one in their right frame of mind is going to drop everything they had going on and include you—I don't care how good you think your stuff may be. Be advised, even though I'm writing from a man's perspective, this reality goes on the other foot as well.

Take a look and see what I'm talking about. You got your bills, and I got mine. I'm not responsible for yours, and you're not responsible for mine. Your bad news isn't my bad news, and mine isn't yours. And, yes, I am always going to pay my mortgage over paying your rent. Yes, I've had that tried on me, and these were my exact words to the young lady: What are we going to do when my house get foreclosed on—downsize to your apartment? No. I don't think so. Needless to say, she is no longer around.

So, a man not helping a woman with her bills has nothing to do with how much he wants to get to know her. It has everything to do with each individual taking care of his/her own until a decision has been made as to whether or not a relationship will take place.

Now, it goes without saying, if someone I'm dating is having trouble and I'm in a position to help, I will. However, I'm not obligated. This is something that's done out of the kindness of someone's heart. Getting to know someone does not require one to lose their mind and allow someone else to put them in a bind they can't recover from. I don't know where this idea came from that a man is supposed to ridiculously spend money he doesn't have to convince a woman how much he care about her. It's superficial and the only thing it proves is he's a fool. Besides, if the truth be told, very few men are in the position to pay for everything.

When I'm confronted with a woman who has a sense of entitlement, it is an insult to my intelligence and it makes me want to vomit. Stop! Stop! Stop! Women who do this, be advised, it's a big turn off, not just for me, but for a lot of men—they just haven't said anything.

Note: In the next section, I have developed an ad women can post when looking for a mate and some good questions they can ask during the interview process.

Classifieds
Husband Wanted

There's no way a woman can gain enough evidence on a man in ninety days to make an informed decision. Even law enforcement take more time than that to build a solid case against their suspect: sometimes it takes years.

Posted Ad: Real Man Wanted

Basic Minimum Requirements: A real lady seeking a career-minded man. He must be faithful, trustworthy, have oats sorted, and no felony convictions. Examples of felony convictions consist of adultery, abandoning your family, and being behind in your child support, etc. Must not have an extensive work history, and no one can sing the song "Papa Was a Rollin' Stone" when they think about you.

Interview Questions

1. Are you seeking a career?
2. Are you willing to sign a contract?
3. Do you have any other prospective employers?
4. How many previous employers have you had?
5. What was the longest position you ever held?
6. What did you like and not like about your previous employer?
7. Have you ever held more than one position at a time?
8. Can you be bonded?
9. Do you have any pending charges against you?
10. Can you provide three good character references?
11. What would your last employer say about you?
12. Have you ever had any MWMs (mishaps while married)?
13. Do you have anything cooking in the burner?

Tips: If you're not accustomed to interviewing someone, here's a few tips for the process. By following these tips, you can get a good idea of one's qualifications for the position you have posted.

- Look them straight in the eyes. If a person can't look you in the eyes, they might be lying.
- Watch their body movement. Do they pat their feet or hands on something? Do they constantly shift in their seat—or do they talk

with their hands? This could be a sign of nervousness about the questions and may mean one is hiding something.

- Observe their response to your questions. Do they pause before answering your question? Do they over-talk, or do they avoid questions by making excuses for not answering? This could mean they're trying to cover up something either past or present—or both.

- Observe the reality of what they're saying to you. Is what they're saying sound like a fairy tale—are they sensationalizing what they're saying? Do they try to make it sound like there's no one else like them, or do they make it sound like they're a gift from God? If so, you're definitely being sold a pipe dream.

- Look for words they use to lend credibility to what they're saying. *Trust me; my word is bond; I keep it 100%; you can take that to the bank and cash it; I don't break my word for nobody*—if you hear this last one, I swear by God, run like hell. You can't trust anything they are saying.

THE PROCESS DESCRIBED above is a matter that should be taken seriously. If performed properly, one should easily be able to assess which candidates will best qualify for the position you have posted. Deciding on a lifetime mate is no joking matter. Therefore, it would behoove one to seek other methods for determining the worthiness of one to be a part of their life. As I have pointed out earlier, what we've been doing is not working. I'm a firm believer in innovation. So, let's be innovative in our quest for that desired mate I hope we all are looking for. Come out of your time capsule and merge your thinking with the signs of the times. We must make a change if we're to restore the commitment to relationships we so desperately need. Don't be afraid. Change is good.

Note: If we're not careful, failing in our relationships can become contagious, and it could affect us in other areas of our lives. It worked like that for me in my life. We need an agent of change.

A Sports Analogy

I F I W E R E a football player and I got drafted to the pros, one of the first things the coach would give me is a team playbook. Within the pages of this team playbook would be all the rules and guidelines a player would need to carry out his responsibilities to the team during the game. As a new player, I would also be given a certain length of time to learn the team's plays and perform them to the coach's standards. If I were unable to perform the plays in the manner prescribed by the coach, I would ultimately be cut from the team. Why? Because I'd have proven myself unwilling to do whatever is needed to learn the plays and help the team be a winner.

It works much the same way with average Christians. They are not willing to do whatever is necessary to learn God's word so they can go out on the field and become a winner. Instead, most Christians rely on worldly crib notes from previous players who have been cut from the team. They are not willing to dip their noses in the Creator's playbook to get the right instructions so they can rightly divide the playbook. This commentary is why we as Christians have the worst batting average of any religious team of today. Regrettably, the average Muslim, Jehovah's Witness, and Jew know the Bible better than those who profess to love Jesus so much—and that's on the up and up. We choose to rely on the preaching of some flamboyant and misinformed preacher who couldn't find their butthole from a hole in the ground instead of allowing God to speak to us through his word. By the way, I do recall one of God's attributes being His ability to speak. This must change if we want to make the team and not get sent home with our bags packed. Don't get cut from the team.

WHAT'S YOUR POLICY?

WHEN COMPARING THE institution of Corporate America to that of Corporate God, there is a vast contrast between the two. For instance, when one invests in the stock of a corporation, one stands the chance of losing their monetary investment. On the other hand, when one invests in a Ponzi scheme carried out by someone in the name of God, one stands the chance of losing their soul.

SATAN'S POLICY

THE ACCUSED BOOK I am adamantly prosecuting has issued stock with an insurance policy that was sold with promises of being fail proof. However, upon careful investigation, it has been revealed that the stock issued amounts to nothing but a Ponzi scheme. This policy's sole purpose is to encourage unsuspecting investors to invest in endeavors with no chance of a return. The true name of this policy is Satan's Policy. It provides the wrong coverage, the wrong insurer, and the wrong administrator. Its core beliefs: who we are, what we have, and where we are going. There is nothing in this policy to include those who invest and believe in this policy, or have a stake in the profits of the company—Claim Rejected.

GOD'S POLICY REIGNS

IF ONE WANTS a money-back guarantee policy, invest in God's policy. You will get the right coverage, the right insurer, and the right administrator. Your investment is 100% refundable if not satisfied. You can check with the relationship Heavenly Host (BBB) and you won't find any complaints. No other insurer has been in existence longer than God. God's practices and methods are open to all who want to see. Only those who are of the contrary reject his policy. And, if you talk to previous investors, they will only have good things to say about God's policy. We cannot change the dress code, love-making code, or marriage code to God's policy. God's way is the only way. GOD'S POLICY APPROVED. The End.

"My people are destroyed for a lack of knowledge...."
(HOSEA 4:6).

COUNT 9

IT'S OKAY TO BE A MAMA'S BOY

*"It's okay to cheat on your wife, but it's
not okay to be a mama's boy."*

WHEN A WOMAN is considering whether or not she will be involved with a man, if I haven't heard this at least a thousand times: I will never marry a mama's boy—my name isn't what it is and the sky isn't over my head. I have heard girlfriends say it, family members say it, been in discussion groups and heard it, and even some of my Christian female friends say they don't want to be involved with a mama's boy. So, what is the problem with a man being a mama's boy?

I intend to prove beyond a shadow of doubt that it is perfectly fine with a man not cutting the spiritual umbilical cord from his mother. In my explanation, I will give biblical, practical, as well as logical reasons to validate my position. I will also demonstrate why women should admire and respect a man who takes care of his mother, and why a woman should never attempt to come between this precious relationship—especially a black man who really loves his mother.

One of the worst things a woman can do is try to put herself on a higher plane than a man's mother. Any attempt of a woman to make a man choose between his mother and his woman will be futile. And more often than not, it will result in his woman being disappointed, frustrated, and feeling abandoned. There's no comparison in the two relationships, and a woman should avoid doing such at all cost.

However, a true woman will appreciate a man's unwavering affection to his mother and never attempt such an insane act. She understands this bond and knows it would be foolish to remotely attempt to pin a man against his mother. A true woman understands she will lose every time. That is, of course, if a man truly loves his mother.

Look at the bright side, if a man truly loves his mother, he is more likely than not to give the same care to his wife. He will be there in his wife's latter years caring for her at every turn. As a matter of fact, a true man won't take his last breath until he has assured his wife is taken care of in his absence. At least that's how it was in the old days. Girlfriends excluded.

I am one hundred percent, absolutely, beyond any doubt, a mama's boy. She will always come first. Anything or anybody who tries to come between us will immediately be sent on their way. She was the first and the last; there was none before her and there will be none after her; besides her, there is no other; she is my Alpha and Omega; my beginning and my end; and I'm absolutely sure she will be my mother until I take my last breath.

Unfortunately, it's not like that with most marriages today. *Maybe, might, possible,* and *as long as the good is good* are appropriate ways to define our level of commitment to today. As a woman told an associate of mine, you're only worth how much money you have. When he told me this, all I could do was laugh. Why? Because it's true in all too many cases.

Here's how I look at this quandary of who should come in first place. Most marriages are recycled and they never stand the test of time. Some of us have been married three or four times—my present company is not excluded. In addition, contrary to God's will, a lot of pastors fit into this commentary as well. Some pastors have been married so many times the church had to do away with the concept of a first lady. It has been replaced with the new concept of the fourth lady. Some of us have kids all over the place. Case in point, some women have kids by five different men—and some men have kids only God can keep count of.

See if this rings a bell. A lot of us have brothers and sisters we didn't even know we had until our latter years. I'm pretty sure you've heard of people not finding out about family members until they were grown. Daddy had another family in another state he keep secret for years. When the song "Papa Was a Rollin' Stone" comes on, most of us can just look in the mirror and know that's our song—women included. And sadly, the man or woman you're sleeping with now might be somebody else's spouse. It's getting quiet up in here.

So, who is your family? Am I your brother? Are you my sister? I don't think those questions were in God's plan. We're getting exactly what we deserve. We can't expect bliss in our marriages when they're not done according to God's plan. He said, as a result of our disobedience, we will have trials and tribulations all the days of our lives. Thorns and thistles shall it bring us. That proclamation is in the beginning of the Bible—the first book. It makes me wonder.

Here's another way I look at it: If I were an investor in relationships, I would conduct a risk–benefit comparison to ascertain which relationship would yield me the most return from my investment. The one with the most reliable and promising return is where I would put the bulk of my investment. In other words, the one with the least risk would be considered the best investment.

RELATIONSHIP INVESTMENT COMPARISON

RELATIONSHIP #1: MOTHER AND SON.

I've been with my mother for fifty years. She's been with me through thick and thin. When I was down and out, she was there; on drugs, she was there; needed a place to stay, she was there; in prison, she was there; through my divorce, she was there; broke, she was there; sick, she was there; jobless, she was there; no food to eat, she was there; no clothes to wear, she was there; purchasing my first house, she was there.

RELATIONSHIP #2: A MAN AND HIS WOMAN.

Now here's comes a woman who has only been around for a few years, who throughout the relationship is never satisfied. She threatens to leave if she doesn't get her way—her kids aren't my kids, the kids are well provided for, hasn't worked since we've been together, can't cook and won't make an attempt to learn how, Mama gets little things while she gets big things and still she complains. From this relationship, here's what I get: a woman with a sense of entitlement. Take that over Mama's good cooking? Some neck-bones and collard greens with some macaroni and cheese and a sweet potato pie for desert. And don't let me forget, a big jaw of Kool-Aid in an old mayonnaise jaw—I don't think so.

This comparison yields a no-brainer decision for me as to which investment I would choose if forced to do so. To put a woman above my mother wouldn't be a good investment to me. The return from my investment with a woman is not worth the risk of me dishonoring Jesus' command from the cross for a man to always take care of his mother. I will not give more credence to a part-time assignment over a full-time assignment. It would be wise for any woman to realize the blessing she has instead of trying to exercise some false powers some fool said she has, which she really doesn't. Heck, I would be better off going to live with my mother and doing like the woman's voice says: go and get a prostitute. Ladies, you don't stand a chance against Mom. Mama got fifty years on you. She already put in her work. You're just beginning the race and complaining already. Enough is enough.

Let's look at the topic of a mama's boy from a biblical perspective on which the woman's voice has no clue. Maybe this will clear up some confusion that is occurring in someone's house:

When Jesus therefore saw his mother, and the disciple standing by, whom he loved, he saith unto his mother, Woman behold thy son! Then saith he to the disciple, behold thy mother! And from that hour that disciple took her unto his own house.

(JOHN 19:26)

Jesus' relationship with his mother was so important to him he commanded his disciple to take care of his mother as blood was rolling down his head. Now that's a son. Dying, and he still made provisions for his mother.

The disciple followed Jesus' command and took care of His mother in spite of the fact that it wasn't his mother. The disciple didn't complain—he didn't say *I can't do it because I have my own family to take care of* or *what is my wife going to say* or *this is too much of a burden for me* or *that's not my mother* and he didn't ask for anything in return. Now that's *"agape love."*

What Jesus, the word manifested in the flesh, was doing is pledging allegiance to one of the Ten Commandments. Jesus' disciple knew exactly where He was coming from:

Honor thy Father and thy mother, as the Lord thy God hath commanded thee; that thy days may be prolonged, and that it may go well with thee. . . .

(DEUTERONOMY 5:16)

Check Mate: Now check this out. I thought that the Old Testament was old and we should sweep it under the rug. But here we have the creator of the dispensation of grace complying with the dispensation of the law. So, if Jesus is obligated to keep the law in the dispensation of grace, shouldn't we? Like I said before, God's laws stand.

A command, folks, isn't optional. He didn't say only if a man is not married, only if a man feels like I it, and only if your wife is okay with it, then put a man's my wife first. So you see, it is God's law, and if a man doesn't comply with the demand of the Creator, there are consequences for being disobedient. It could mean a grave illness or even death. (Read the last portion of Deuteronomy 5:16.)

Moreover, not only was Jesus complying with the Ten Commandments, he was also adhering to the customs of his people. It was customary in those days for the firstborn son to take the headship of the family in the absence of the father. In addition, once the father reached a certain age, the firstborn son was to assume the headship of the family—even if he had his own wife and children. Even though most men aren't aware they're practicing this custom, it's innately within us to do so.

Furthermore, this principle follows another command that was rich in biblical days: *"But if any provide not for his own, and specially for those of his own house, he hath denied the faith, and is worse than an infidel"* (1 Timothy 5:8). In other words, if a man fails to take care his mother, he is in a worse position than a non-believer. That's pretty bad. And don't confuse the words "his own" to mean his wife and kids only.

I always wondered why the Savior of all mankind never in His most crucial hour at no time mumbled a word about a relationship between a man and a woman. I believe it's because Jesus, being God manifested in the flesh, looked into the cup at the Garden of Gethsemane and saw the degenerated state of the marriages we have today—they are deplorable. His heart must have been crushed to see He was dying for people who wouldn't be faithful to the first institution His Father created. He knew husbands would be cheating on their wives and leaving them left and right, wives would be cheating on their husbands, and woman would be sleeping with two and three men at a time—and he knew pastors would lead the way in the smearing of God's institution of marriage.

Furthermore, Christ, coming through a pure woman, understood the bond and the pureness of a relationship between a mother and her son. Unlike most relationships between a man and his wife, a relationship between a man and his mother is undefiled, unconditional, forever, and not based on anything superficial. It is not based on "what have I done for you lately?" Nor does it swing whichever way the wind is blowing for the day. It remains until death do us part.

Moreover, Mama suffered—you didn't. She's going to always be there—maybe you'll be there. She asks for little things—you complain and get big things. She cooks—you won't touch a frying pan. She knows her son loves her—a husband must prove his love to his wife every second of the day. It's easy to please a mother—nothing a lot of husbands do pleases their wives. Mother keeps family matters at home—you take them to the street. You decide.

THE WOMB THEORY

W HEN A MAN is in his mother's womb, there is no other relationship that will remotely come close to the intimacy he shares with his mother. During this process, a man's mother is his life-source. His total survival depends on her. She is his shelter—she nourishes him, checks on him both day and night, and will protect him even at the risk of her own life. As a result of such undying love, contrary to popular belief, a man's umbilical cord may be physically severed from his mother, but it will never be spiritually, emotionally, or psychologically severed. A man will always thirst for the comfort and love only a mother can bring. If a woman doesn't understand and accept this concept for what it is, she will continue to bang her head against the wall and be frustrated all her awaking days.

When all else fails, I often find myself retreating to my mother's house, and my heart instantly begins to sing. Any hurt, anger, disappointment, or pain I am feeling immediately subsides. I know I have reached a place where what I have, who I am, and where I'm going is of no relevance. My mother always says to me, "If you're happy, then I'm happy." And I will in turn say to her, "Mom, if you're happy, then I'm happy." This is our way of saying, "No matter what it takes, I will do it to make you happy."

In closing to this count, my sisters, I know some of you are going to get offended by what I'm about to say, but it is exactly how I feel. And if you're anything like me, you would prefer the truth over a lie any day.

I don't care if I never have illegal sex with a woman again: you will not come before my mother under no circumstances. I don't care if you're my wife, brother, sister, or whatever relationship it may be, no one will come before my mother. If I am relegated to spending the rest of my life with my mother, I will be the happiest man in the world. I know many men have made some women believe their stuff is the greatest thing since sliced bread, but I'm here to tell you it will never match a mother's love—nor will it stand the test of time. There's just no comparing the two loves. A man's mother has the best goodies in the world he will ever taste. Believe me when I say that.

Understand this, my sisters: If you don't take anything else away from this discourse, know that a real man has a special place in his heart for everyone in his life. He has a place for his mother, wife, children, and the rest of his family. No one can occupy the space of another. He will do everything within his power to assure his entire family is satisfied. And if he falls down, he will get up and keep trying until he accomplishes his mission. That's a real man. So, stop complaining about things of little importance, take a look around, and see the many blessing he has already provided for you. Especially if he's coming home every night and not cheating on you.

Fact: What woman on earth can claim her stuff is better than Mama's—none. IT'S OKAY TO BE A MAMA'S BOY!

IF HE'S MEETING YOUR KIDS BEFORE YOU HAVE A RING AND HAVE SET A DATE, IT'S TOO SOON

IN AN EARLIER count of this case, I shared with you my feelings in regard to a woman meeting my mother and daughter. So, I'm not going to waste your time with a rehashing of an event already spoken on. However, I will tell you this: The reasons for me not allowing a woman to meet my family too soon have nothing to do with the reasons mentioned by Steve Harvey.

In addition, I also spoke on the differences between a man and a boy. Again, it would be pointless to address this matter again. If one's memory need refreshing, one can reread the sections "Boys Like to Hunt" and "A Mama's Boy." However, I am going to discuss with you from a biblical, practical, and a psychological perspective the dangers of introducing your kids to a man too soon. And the truth of the matter is this: There are real dangers when introducing your child to a strange mate too early.

Ladies and gentlemen, don't take the well-being of your child for granted, especially at the counsel of someone whose word you can't trust before it is spewed out of their mouth.

CHILD PSYCHOLOGY 101

FIRST, IF ONE were to consult a child psychologist on the matter of introducing your child to your mate, one would be informed of the confusion a child experiences from having a strange man or woman suddenly thrown into their life. This confusion stems from a child's inability to process this new information and their lack of familiarity in dealing with sudden changes. Children must be given time to adjust to the idea of impeding changes. If not, look out.

Causing a sudden change in a child's brain can result in a violent reaction that gives the false impression that the child doesn't like the party being introduced—a false-negative reaction—but that may be the furthest thing from the truth.

One must keep in mind a child's brain is underdeveloped, and a nurturing process is required for the proper adjustment. They're deficient in experiential knowledge of such matters. Therefore, children must be given time to adapt to their new situation.

When encountered with this situation, it would be wise for one to gradually bring the child into this new idea and give them the time to adjust. The early introduction is not to take place in the early stages of a friendship. Get a ring on your finger and set a date first. Your child doesn't need to be caught up in grown-folk mess. If one wants to be the freak of the week, that's your business, just keep it away from God's precious little ones.

Memory Lane: Remember, ninety days isn't enough time to build a case against someone. So, when it comes to your child, ninety days isn't enough time to determine if your prospective mate will be good for you and your child. Further, from a biblical perspective, we are to teach our children in the way they should go: *"Train up a child in the way he should go; and when he is old, he will not depart from it"* (Proverbs 22:6).

We are to be a good example for our children. Show them the right and wrong way to do things. Teach them the proper way of merging two families together. And when they are of age and have children of their own, they will do the same.

Think on this: If we constantly introduce our children to everyone we meet, we may give our children the impression that it's okay to have more than one mate at a time. On the flip side, why introduce your child to someone if you are not sure they will be around the next day? It makes absolutely no sense and can only be detrimental to the child. Hell, with our record on relationships, one could go through ten to twenty potential mates before they meet Mr. or Mrs. Right. If you think I don't know what I am talking about, take out a pencil and piece of paper and mark down the number of mates you went through to get the one you wanted. That is, if you have the one you want.

I can't tell anyone how to raise their children; however, I will say this: it would be advisable for one to consider the well-being of their child. So, with that said, my sisters and brothers, take serious heed to the warning below.

Warning: My sisters, if you bring your man home, take him in your bedroom, and knock boots while your fifteen-year-old daughter is in the house, and she hears you making all that noise, what do you think she's going to do when she gets the chance? Let me answer that for you. She's going to do the same thing. Why? Because you showed her how to knock boots, and it sounded like you were having a lot of fun doing it. So, when you come home and catch Little Johnny pounding on your daughter, don't get mad at her because she is only doing what you taught her—fathers, that goes for you too.

Be advised, when parents who perform in front of their children in that manner are trying to figure out how their children got there themselves, they should do like Michael Jackson said, take a look at the man or woman in the mirror—and that's where they'll find the answer. I know I'm right.

As I stated earlier, Jesus gave children more credit than we are willing to give them today. He understood that children had the ability to comprehend things beyond what some could imagine. So, when you are doing your dirt and don't think your child knows what is going on, I just stopped by to let you know that you're sadly mistaken; they are fully aware. Your children have a watchful eye on Mom and Pop looking for guidance—you're their ultimate role model.

The care of children is the responsibility of the parents and one that shouldn't be taken lightly. Let's go back to times past and watch what we do around our children. There is a time and a place for everything. And a man meeting a woman's child before she has a ring and has set a date is not the time, and there is no place.

Practice What I Preach: I took the care of my daughter to heart when she was being raised. Let me share a real-life incident that took place while my daughter was in my care and my ex-wife was standing alongside.

We were standing on the bus stop in downtown Baltimore waiting for the bus to go home. A friend of my ex-wife came along and they began to chat. As I stood there listening, I held my daughter tightly in my arms protecting her from the elements. Shortly after her arrival, my ex-wife's friend requested to see my daughter, but I was reluctant. It was cold outside and I didn't want our newborn to be exposed to the weather. I hesitated to show her my daughter and my wife gave me a look like *don't you embarrass me*. So, I succumbed to the request, thinking that a look would suffice. However, when I uncovered our daughter's face for a second, the friend leaned in to kiss my daughter. I quickly pulled my daughter out of her reach. She was shocked and my ex-wife's jaws dropped to the ground. I didn't give a good hoot. As I began to walk away, the bus came and we boarded to continue our journey home. While on the bus, my ex-wife questioned me as to why I pulled my daughter away and embarrassed her. She said I didn't have to do that because her friend didn't mean any harm. I explained to her that I knew the woman didn't mean any harm, but we were responsible for our child's health, so nothing could be taken for granted. I went further to say, "Even though that's your so-called friend, you don't know what she might have, and I don't want her transferring it to our baby." After explaining this to her, a light went off and her frustration with me subsided.

You see, folks, what appears to be harmless can result in devastating consequences for our children. If a kiss can bring life-threatening affects to your child, imagine what a deranged man you've only known for ninety days can do. Personally, I don't want to think about the possibilities.

Spare Me Please: Every time I watch a news report of some woman's boyfriend she hardly knew killing her innocent child, a piece of me dies, and my mind conjures extremely harsh punishments for the perpetrator. These instances weigh so heavily on me they seem to shorten my lifespan. So, do me a favor and stop killing me day by day out of your desperation to have a man in your child's life. I would rather see you raise that child alone than to have to face a tragedy that will haunt you for the rest of your life. Be patient and wait on the Lord. He will renew your strength. Now, let the truth be told.

I AIN'T YOUR BABY'S DADDY

TOO MANY WOMEN are so desperate to have a man in their children's lives they will hook up with the first thing flying with a zipper to play Daddy. In addition, society is so off course when it comes to the roles of those merging two families together, I can only pray that this trend doesn't get any worse. It is frightening to me to see the lack of cognizance with regard to this matter.

Truth Unveiled. Hold on, my sisters, for reality is about to slap you smack dead in the face. You're about to get it like you've never heard it before. The record must be set straight. Let me say it again in case you didn't hear me the first time: "I AIN'T YOUR BABY'S DADDY."

It is believed by too many women that when a man gets involved with a woman with kids he's entering into a package deal that includes assuming the financial responsibility for another man's children. Wrong! I don't know where in the world some women get this idea that a man is supposed to take care of their children in order to be with them. That responsibility lies with the man whose loins that child came from.

Foolishly, too many men fall into this trap laid for them by some women who have been misinformed as to a man's responsibility to their children when they're involved in an intimate relationship. To add insult to injury, unfortunately, in many cases, a lot of men caught in this web of deception end up neglecting their own children to play Daddy for someone else's children. Homey don't play that! They fail to pay their child support; the mother has to beg them for help; they never come see their children; and some even try to get some when they do decide to pay a visit once a year. That's not a White Man's problem or the New Jim Crow. That's a Black Man's problem and the new Black Crow.

Be informed. There is no such thing as a step-daddy, substitute daddy, or a replacement daddy. The man a woman laid down with to have that child is the daddy. He's responsible for the financial care of his own. There is nothing in the archives of dating that binds a man to the financial responsibility of another man's child. In addition, I've never read anything in the Bible stating that God obligates a man to take care of another man's child and if he didn't, God would be upset with him.

Furthermore, I'm not trying to step in for another man—I can't take the place for the real thing. I'm not trying to substitute for another man—no one wants an imitation. And I'm not trying to replace another man—children can spot a knockoff a mile away. I fully understand my role when it comes to me dating a woman with children. I am Mr. James, Mama's husband. No more and no less. That's okay with me.

Look at it another way: A woman who has kids and is involved with a man that's not their father—she can't take him downtown for child support; she can't call him an absentee dad; she can't call him an unfit dad; and her children can't say he was just a seed. None of these descriptions I've heard kids use when they're talking about their MIA dad would be fitting for a man who is not responsible for them.

What happened to the days when the titles of Mr. and Mrs. carried just as much authority as Reverend? Back in the day, Mother made it clear to her children that Mr. James was her husband and not her children's father. And the children would respect him regardless of how they felt about him. And, if they got out of line, Mama didn't have a problem going upside their head with whatever see got a hold of and putting them back in line. Mama's husband never had to say a mumbling word. Mama also understood it wasn't his job to provide for her kids and was grateful for everything he did. She didn't have a sense of entitlement like a lot of women do today. As a result of mother's attitude, the man was more willing to go far and beyond what she expected of him. In other words, she got more than what she bargained for.

Here's something else for women to think about: If you're involved with a man, he marries you, and moves you and your kids from a cramped two-bedroom apartment to his nice five-bedroom house, he's already taking care of your children. In fact, your children may be getting something his own children don't have: a father figure. Not to mention food, shelter, clothing, continued guidance, and the comfort of knowing there's a man around to assist with the protection of the family.

In addition, anyone with half a brain would know that if any decent man is in a house with children, he's not going to see them go without, not if he can help it—even if they're not his kids. The mother won't have to demand anything because the family's humble spirit will win him over every time.

I firmly believe that some women who institute this school of thought are flying under the radar to disguise the true intent of their wanting to be with a man—that's a Trick-and-John relationship. Here's how it works: You take care of my children, and you'll get the benefit of the goodies. This type of relationship certainly falls in line with the protocols of a trade-for-a-trade relationship.

I believe this mentality is born by women who believe they're doing the man a favor by having sex with him. Somewhere along the way, someone has told them a woman's body is worth more than that of a man's—on a higher plateau. Therefore, he should be willing to pay for her stuff by taking care of her kids. That's a lie. To me, it sounds like a man who is in this situation has found himself what I have termed a live-in prostitute. My belief is this: After we have illegal sex with one another, we're even. Where do we go from here? Once again, an even exchange isn't no robbery. I got mine and you got yours, a favor for a favor—we're even-Steven, baby. And if a woman feels like she didn't get hers, I suggest she find someone she can break even with.

PROSTITUTE–JOHN RELATIONSHIP IDENTIFIERS

▶ If a woman has her hand stuck out for money every time you see her, you're dealing with a prostitute.

▶ If a woman asks you for money for something right after every time you have sex with her, you're dealing with a prostitute.

▶ If a woman tells you she can only come see you if you buy her some gas, more likely than not, you're in a Prostitute–John relationship.

▶ If a woman is okay with you not taking care of your own kids, you're probably in a Prostitute–John relationship.

▶ If a woman believes a man is supposed to pay for everything, there's a good chance you're in a Prostitute–John relationship.

▶ If a woman tells you how much money her previous man spent on her, I'm almost certain you're in a Prostitute–John relationship.

▶ If a woman sings a song to you that clearly suggests she will give you her goodies in exchange for you paying her bills, you're most certainly in a Prostitute–John relationship.

▶ If a woman questions being with you because you can't buy her lavish things she sees other men buying for their mates, you should know by now what time it is.

- If a woman thinks you're supposed to let her go all Willy Silly with the money she makes, and you're supposed to kill yourself trying to keep up with the bills, you know what you got on your hands.

- If a man can set his watch by the due date of his woman's bills, you know what it is.

- If a woman thinks her only responsibility is to lay on her back, it goes without saying.

- If your woman tells you to make sure you leave the money on the dresser, we all know what that's about.

- If a woman is sleeping with a man she doesn't like just because . . . it doesn't take a rocket scientist to figure that out.

- If a woman allows a man to do anything he wants to her sexually because he's paying the bills, even a blind man can see what that's about.

- If a woman is with a man under the disguise of security, the handwriting is on the wall.

BE ADVISED, ALL women don't fit this mode. As I stated earlier in this case, and as the evidence in the next presentation will reveal, a lot of women are capable of handling their own business—that includes taking care of their own children. As a matter of fact, some women do it better than a lot of men. This fact seems to be a problem for some men who feel threatened by the independence of some women. Their ego tells them they will be less than a man if a woman is able to financially provide for the family over the man.

In my finale to this count, we should stop allowing others to decide for us who is best for us—especially our children. This is our decision alone. We're the parent. I'm totally against the theory of introducing kids to mates early in the game. One must do their due diligence before one brings someone into the home. And that's a fact.

COUNT 11

THE MARK OF THE HIGH CALLING

I press towards the mark of the high calling of God in Christ Jesus.
—PHILIPPIANS 3:14

IN MY FIFTY years here on earth, it has always been my understanding that most women, especially Christian women, have a goal—a destination, a mark—they are trying to reach when it comes to relationships. Typically, that mark is to ultimately get married and live happily ever after.

Seeing that marriage is the first institution mandated by God, it is an honorable goal for anyone to have. Unfortunately, because of the changes made to God's laws on marriage, the chances of one reaching their mark and enjoying the satisfaction of achieving a life-long desire will be missed by a lot of women—their chances are slim to none—especially a Holy Matrimony.

After careful evaluation of the defendant's manuscript, it is the prosecution's opinion that the defendant has an enormous amount of admiration for men who are able to have multiple women—even when they're married. To prove this fact, at this time, the prosecution would like to submit into evidence his writings that show his propitious attitude towards those who indulge in the pimp lifestyle, and shun the thought of marriage without any hesitation. Once viewed, the evidence will clearly show there is no denying of his approval and affection for a heathenish lifestyle. Take a look.

In an opening statement to his book, the defendant explained his experience when he first got to Hollywood. He wondered why so many beautiful woman would attach themselves to a man when they knew they were just a part of a string. His fascination was so great with the pimp lifestyle, it appeared as if he was living it himself. Such a huge fascination with this particular lifestyle will make anyone want to go. . . . The handwriting is so clearly printed on the wall—even a fifth-grader could see it.

The defendant explained that these characters were able to accomplish this because of who they were, what they had, and where they were going. This is the same analogy he used to explain to women that a man would not commit to a relationship until he accomplished the aforementioned things. In other words, if a man achieves the same things as his role models, women would want to attach themselves to him, and he can do as he pleases. Women would want to be a bead on a string and just fit into the cracks of the man's life.

Ladies, take a hard look at the following scriptures to see what you're really getting yourself into when you follow the advice of the unlearned: *"For as he thinketh in his heart, so is he: Eat and drink saith he to thee; but his heart is not with thee"* (Proverbs 23:7).

Satan used this same reasoning in his futile attempt to persuade the master:

> *Again, the devil taketh him up into an exceeding high mountain, and showeth him all the kingdoms of the world, and the glory of them. And saith unto him, All these things will I give thee, if thou wilt fall down and worship me.*
>
> (MATTHEW 4:8–9)

Listen to what Satan was really saying to Jesus and see if it sounds familiar. Jesus, look man, who I am, what I have, and where I'm going can be all yours if you marry me and do what I tell you to do. Just bow down to me and worship me and you can have all that I have—because I'm the man.

I will profess my love for you, provide for you, and protect you. And if you just sit there and look pretty, the only thing you will have to do is give me the cookie when I want and how I want. And you should be happy to be with me so you can fit into the crack of my life or be a bead on my string.

Ladies, just like you, for Jesus to have succumbed to the things of the world would have been giving the devil power over Him—your man. He would've conceded to the things that are worldly that can only bring worldly satisfaction—absent peace. Just like Satan would've done to Jesus, every chance your man gets he will throw what he's done for you in your face. *I bought you a new car, so I want the thing. I pay your bills, so what's up with the thing? I'm the man, so what's up with the thing? If you don't give me the thing, I'll go get it from somewhere else, so what's up with the thing?* No ring, no thing—that's the main thing.

The Mountain Top: Ain't no mountain high enough for a woman to degrade herself and replace the honorable things of God. We all know that one day you're up—and the next day you're down. We also know that when the materialism of a marriage goes—there goes the marriage. So get some of God's Crazy Glue so your marriage will stay together.

Let me be very clear: The women being described in the defendant's introductory scenario are gold diggers. In other words, he's describing high-class whores and prostitutes—if there's any such thing. By the way, whoredom is no phenomenon: neither is it relegated to women.

As I stated earlier in this book, a lady would never base her decision to be with a man only on materialism. A man's character will and should be at the top of her agenda, and there's only one bead on his string—hers.

Don't get me wrong. I'm not saying a woman should just accept any-thing—nobody wants a bum. We all want someone with ironclad goals. As a matter of fact, most sensible women want someone they feel secure about being able to provide for them if they need it—and there's nothing wrong with that. However, a man's financial position shouldn't be the deciding factor as to whether a woman chooses to be with him or not—that's all

I'm saying. There are so many other questions a woman should ask before getting involved with someone.

INTERVIEW QUESTIONS

1. Does he believe in God? In other words, does he know more than three scriptures?
2. Does he practice what he preaches and come through on his promises?
3. Does he believe in sex before marriage? (Watch his face and observe the timeliness of his response.)
4. Will he take a test for sexually transmitted diseases before marriage? (A man who cares about his health just as much as you won't refuse.)
5. Does he read or study the Bible? If the answer is "read," you know what you're dealing with: a pretender. He will go to church with you until he gets what he wants. Then, it's back to the club with his boys.
6. What kind of relationship does he have with his mother? This is extremely important. It could be a good indication as to how he would treat you.
7. Does he go to strip clubs? If the answer is yes, he's still filled with lust. You're not the object of his affection. It won't work.
8. How many wives has he had so far? If the answer is two or more, look out, he's not likely to stick around— you better at least be wondering.
9. How many baby mamas does he have? If the answer is more than one, there's no commitment in him. He likes to spread himself thin. Don't be his next victim.
10. Have you ever been married? If he's a certain age and has never been married, you should wonder why.
11. Does he help out in his community? If not, he only cares about himself. Life is a community effort.

12. When was the last time he voted? If he says it's a waste of time to vote, he doesn't care what happens to him or his people.

THE QUESTIONS LISTED above, if presented to a man at the optimum time, will help a woman gage whether a man is worth her time or not. They will at the very least help a woman understand the mindset of that particular man. Be advised, these questions are not all inclusive. They are used as an example to motivate women to be inquisitive about the prospective man in their lives. One should develop their own questions based on what is important to them—and only you know you best.

I believe the number-one indication of a man's worthiness of a relationship is his relationship with God. If a man is right in his relation with God, his conscience will compel him to perform his family duties according to God's standards—and I'm not talking about the normal lip service of some men. I'm talking about tangible evidence a woman can see for herself. This is the intersection where actions meet words.

My sisters, this next commentary should be looked at very closely. It served me no pleasure to have this revealed to me. As a matter of fact, it brought my heart sadness and made me wonder if I contributed to this dilemma. I'm sure in some way I did. Nonetheless, it must be shared with you. Take a look.

AVERAGE WOMAN VERSUS PROSTITUTE

FOOD FOR THOUGHT: When considering to be involved with someone, a woman and a prostitute both have a goal. A prostitute's goal is to receive some type of monetary reward for her services. On the other end of the spectrum, a typical woman's goal is to ultimately be married to the man she's involved with.

I'm sad to say, in one sense, I have more respect for the prostitutes of the world than the average woman. Why? If this were an election, the prostitutes would be winning by a landslide. The prostitutes get their mark upfront before the man gets what he wants. As a result, men who are familiar with the etiquette of dealing with a prostitute know in order to get what they want they must come to the table with the money contract in hand. If not, they will be sent on their way. A prostitute won't even take off her clothes until the John forks over the dough. They've learned from their mistakes and refuse to take a man at his word and get burned.

On the other hand, however, the average woman will put the cart before the horse every time based on a pipe dream. She keeps listening to empty promises and never achieves her goal. She gives her goodies up with nothing etched in stone and, thus, keeps getting burned over and over again—only to come up empty handed. Some women give him the whole farm: the cow, the milk, the chickens, and the hens. The man turns around and writes a check that is returned with NSM written on it (Non-Sufficient Man). To top it off, he leaves you with the children and you have to beg him for help. Even crazier, some men have the nerve to take care of the other woman's children before they take care of their own. If you think that's crazy, some women are so desperate they have the nerve to take him back after the other woman gets finish with him.

My sisters, here's what I'm saying to some of you: To keep doing the same thing over and over again and expecting different results is insanity. Wake up out of your stupor! Give up the penis-envy addiction for the God-love addiction. Get your contract signed, sealed, and delivered by God's notary service.

TEST DRIVE

MY SISTERS, HOW many men are you going to allow to test drive you before you put your foot down? If you keep issuing out test drives, by the time you meet a serious buyer, your engine will have a class-three leak and you will be considered a lemon. As a result, no one will want to invest their time, energy, and money into an engine that is on the brink of blowing—your bottom is about to fall out.

Let's look at this under a different light. If you go to purchase a car, the salesman is only going to take you around the block a time or two before you have to make a decision. After the test drive, he will be standing there with his pen and contract in hand waiting for you to sign—that is, of course, if your credit is good. If you don't sign, you won't be going on another test drive.

Now, look at why the salesman wanted you to take a test drive. When the salesman saw you walk into the dealership, his whole mission was to get you to sit in the car. Why? He knew his car was a good thing, and if he got you to drive it, he knew you would fall in love with that car and would want to keep it—it happened to me. A pack of wild horses couldn't get me out of that car.

Here's what I'm saying to you: If you know your goodies are like snap, crackle, and pop—like Lays Potato Chips, you can't just eat one—stop issuing out test drives to your glorious car. Perform a background check first. Check out his credit rating; check out his work history; do a baby-to-Mama equity ratio; make sure he has a valid license to drive; see how many repossessions he's had in the past; and, for God's sake, make him sign his name on the dotted line before you hand over to him the key to your highway to heaven.

Take it to the Streets

L ET ME GIVE you another example to illustrate when a tester is needed or not by using a darker side of my life. When I was much younger and participated in the drug game, we used to give out samples of a new product to drug addicts to see how good the product was. We would get word out that we would be giving out samples of our new product soon—never a time or a place. The drug addicts would be anxiously waiting for the show down.

When the time arrived, we would go to a certain area to distribute our testers. Upon our arrival, once spotted, a crowd would ensue and we would take a hand full of samples and throw them in the crowd. The drug addicts would fight and scramble to get a sample. They would push one another, dive on the ground, and some would even try to snatch the sample out of another's hand. When the dust settled, we would just sit back and wait for the report to come in. If the report was good, the product sold. Hence, every drug addict in town would want to get some.

On the flip side, when we knew we had a good product, no samples were given out. They could beg, pled, or cry. No matter what they did, they weren't getting any until they paid for it. Come hell or high water, if they wanted what we had, they had to pay for it. So what's the report on your stuff? Is it good or bad? Has it lost its savor or not? Do you need to give out samples? Will the male addict fight over you? Be real with yourself—because only you know the answer.

Ladies, if you know your product is good, why do you continue to issue out samples? Close shop and place a "Not for Sale" sign on your door. Make all interested parties aware that your stuff is for marriage—one must have a contract to gain entry. Followed by—Absolutely No Exceptions. Issue out a disclaimer to the traditional thought that it is necessary to test the waters first.

Note: The next section is not to degrade, demean, or place anyone in a particular class. It is specifically designed to make us think about our ways—men included. We should be open to anything that would help us in our efforts to have a successful relationship.

HOOKER THRESHOLD

- ► You lose your virginity. No, you're not a hooker. Everybody makes mistakes.
- ► You rebel against your parents and give in again. No. You're just young and dumb.
- ► You get in high school and start feeling yourself. All of the boys are chasing you and you slip up again. No. This should've been your wake-up call.
- ► You get in college and you really think you're a woman now. You got the star basketball player after you; you don't want to disappoint him, so you give in. You're on the fifteen yard line.
- ► You graduate from college, get married, and then find out your husband cheated on you, and you go buck wild. You're on the ten yard line.
- ► You start sleeping with your boss. You're on the five yard line.
- ► You start clubbing and taking men home from the club. You've just scored a touchdown and crossed into the hooker end zone.

YOUR SEXUAL EXPERIENCE may not have driven down this road. However, I think you get the point. This illustration was simply to get one to take a look into their soul. It is not meant to judge anyone or determine one's worth. It is meant to have one take a look in the mirror and consider the fault of one's ways, and maybe we can prevent some young man or young woman from going down the same path.

SEE FOR YOURSELF

P EOPLE ALWAYS SAY if a person has goals and wants to get a clear picture of the direction they're going in, put it on paper. So, to see what I am talking about, I challenge you to take an index card and write down every person you've had intimate relations with, and you will see what I'm talking about. After you finish, multiply that number by ten, and you will get your product. Don't be ashamed of the results of this test. This is God's Emergency Alert System. This is only a test.

Be encouraged. If you've failed this test, know there is always room for improvement. I am not excluded from this test, nor am I exempted from preaching against this lifestyle just because I'm guilty as charged. I must preach against this lifestyle because I know the damaging affects it can have on one's life. There's an old saying: "Some must die that others may live." I'm talking about saving our children.

I like to think of myself as a relatively intelligent man. I can articulate my goals in a way that would appear to be sound to most logical people. However, my sincerity for my goals is a matter that remains to be seen. Furthermore, having goals and being able to articulate them is no indication of a man's worthiness of being in a relationship, nor does it mean a man wants a woman in his goals just because he went out on a few dates with her and they had illegal sex together—that's what the woman's voice means by "In Too Deep." As usual, God has something to say about this topic in His questions to ask.

In a previous section, I identified several characteristics needed for a leader. The one I would like to call to mind is followership. This characteristic is used by the military as the primary trait needed for one to be a leader. Christ used this same criteria to determine those who are worthy of being in His army. As such, the ability of a boy to transition into a man depends on his willingness to follow and whom he is following. Is he following a father who is still a boy, is he following the television, or is he just going with the flow? So, let's see what the defendant believes a man will do to assist a woman in reaching her mark.

He stated that his son will do the same things those he admires so much do, simply because he can and women will allow him. I wonder why? This attitude sounds to me like a father patting his son on the back for taking a girl's virginity. However, I'm not surprised—one can only teach what one knows. And as the saying goes, "The apple never falls far from the tree." So ask yourself this: where does a boy get his morals from?

Breaking News: To force a female to have sex against her will is rape—there's no two ways about it. Young women are raped every day by the lust within boys their father's eagerly placed in them, and pat them on the back for acting on. *Did you hit that, son? She know your name—that's my boy.* No, that's your rapist. If the blind continue to lead the blind, we will never restore the dignity to families we so desperately need.

In my lifetime, through their writings, I have been blessed to be exposed to some of the greatest minds this side of heaven. As a result, I have learned that one's ability to think is of paramount importance. Why am I saying this? For a woman to assume that she will have a good relationship with a man because he had one with his mother is not guaranteed—I hope I'm wrong. Look at it this way: Most men view their relationship with their mother and wife as two separate entities. Therefore, their approach will be different. Think about all of the horrible stories we hear about men who had a great relationship with their mother but treat their wives like a dog. On the flip side, some men may deem their mother's worthy of a status above their wives—but that doesn't mean he will treat a woman like a dog.

At this juncture in the refutation of this sorry excuse for a book, I feel compelled to share with my readers the feelings I am experiencing at this time. In all my years of reading I have never read a book that has brought such condescension to me. The more I read this book, the more difficult it becomes to finish reading it. It's sad to see someone who professes to know and love God show such blatant disregard for protecting the creation God has provided for us. Don't be mistaken; the disdain I'm experiencing is not only with this book, but also with our degenerated state of being as black men. If you ask any doctor, lawyer, judge, coroner, or mortician if certain cases rip their hearts out, the answer will be yes. This is one of those cases for me. I can only imagine God's heart is crying at this time. The mark for all people should be marriage. There's nothing better than when two people come together and forge a relationship in Holy Matrimony. We must turn back the hands of time and return to our first love.

My brothers, we must be the ones on the front line leading the charge in the restoration of our women to their rightful status. If we don't, no one else will. The whole world is watching the original king to see how he honors his woman so they can gauge how to treat her. My sisters, stop being a test dummy for every Joe want-to-be that comes around. Know that you are a queen and deserve to be treated as such. If you set your mark to God's mark you will never go wrong.

THE RIGHT WAY VERSUS THE WRONG WAY

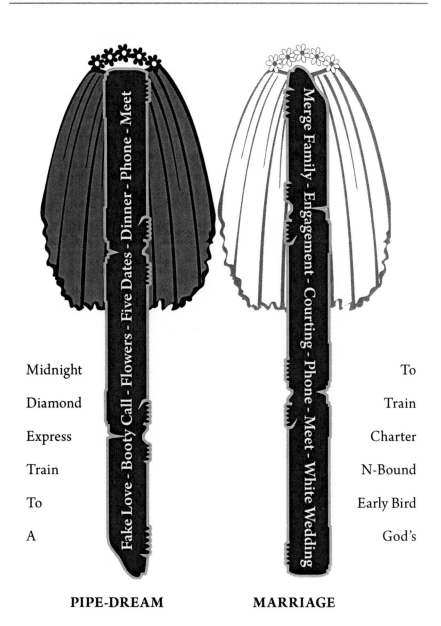

Midnight Diamond Express Train To A

Fake Love - Booty Call - Flowers - Five Dates - Dinner - Phone - Meet

Merge Family - Engagement - Courting - Phone - Meet - White Wedding

To Train Charter N-Bound Early Bird God's

PIPE-DREAM   **MARRIAGE**

WHICH TRAIN ARE YOU BOARDING?

THE OWNER'S MANUAL

TYPICALLY, WHENEVER A manufacturer of goods produces a product that requires the consumer to assemble the product once at home, an owner's manual will be included in the packaging to assist the consumer with the proper assembly process. Once assembled, if the consumer experiences any problems with the product, the owner's manual will serve as a guide to find a solution to the problem being experienced. If the owner is unable to determine a corrective measure for the problem, she/he will return the product to the manufacturer to be fixed or exchanged.

It is important for one to understand why the consumer returns the product to the manufacturer and not some jack-legged or shade-tree mechanic. Here's why:

The manufacturer conceptualized, designed, and assembled all of the parts. In other words, the manufacturer was there in the beginning, middle, and end. The manufacturer knows all the ins and outs associated with the product—those little intricacies that your cousin June Bug will never give detail to. In addition, when the manufacturer designed the parts of the product, the parts were designed with very specific and detailed specifications. As a result, the tools needed to properly repair the product are possessed by the manufacturer and the manufacturer only. That's something a mechanic will never reveal—her/his inability to do the job the right way, the first time.

It works exactly the same way when it comes to relationships. God is the manufacturer of relationships. He formed, created, designed, and assembled relationships together. He was there in the beginning, middle, and end. He knows the parts of His creation, the specifications of the tools required to fix His creation, and all the nooks and crannies that are hidden from our friends and family. And when His product returns to His shop for repairs, it leaves as good as new: Your hands will look new—and your feet will too. Most importantly, He has never failed to successfully repair a product, and His work is one-hundred-percent guaranteed.

So, with the oddsmakers on God's side, why are we resorting to the so-called relationship experts who couldn't find their bottom-end from a hole in the ground? Is it because they sound good? Is it because they're famous and think that lends them credibility? Is it because they have fancy letters behind their names and someone told them they have the tell-all answer for all relationships? Do they think their wisdom is above God's? Or are we just so gullible that we are willing to listen to any fly-by-night relationship expert that comes along? I'll let my readers decide for themselves where they stand. Now, keep in mind, everyone is not duped by the cloak of intelligence.

In closing, I believe the reason so many people fall into the clutches of the fancy talkers can be found in the thoughts of some of our society's great thinkers.

GREAT THINKERS

I.   The Bible says, "My people perish because of a lack of knowledge." In addition, it also states, "So a man thinks in his heart, so is he."

II. The United Negro College Fund puts it this way: "A mind is a terrible thing to waste."

III. Dr. Cornell West puts it this way: "The reason we have such mediocre public officials is because the great thinkers of society enter the private sector instead of the public sector."

I CONCUR WITH EACH of the aforementioned statements. Why? It appears to me that the art of thinking has been abandoned, only to be replaced by a world view—from raising our children to marriage. If the world is doing it, then that means it's okay to do. This is an extremely sad commentary, especially for Christians.

People, I'm not saying there aren't other sources one can use to assist them with their relationship problems. But at the very least, we as Christians should make God's ownership manual our first selection. Let the church say amen!

COURT IS NOW IN RECESS!

CPSIA information can be obtained at www.ICGtesting.com
Printed in the USA
LVOW11s0856160916

504814LV00001B/19/P